SHEDS IN CAMERA

Plate 1: A work-stained Large Prairie, No. 8100, poses in classic 'rods down' fashion beside the coaling plant at its home shed, Leamington, on 28th July 1962. The coal stage is a typical model provided for a Churchward straight shed: 32ft. × 30ft. in brick, topped by an 8ft.-high tank, holding 45,000 gallons of water.

T. W. Nicholls

SHEDS IN CAMERA

ROGER GRIFFITHS

Oxford Publishing Co.

INTRODUCTION

The development of the GWR's engine sheds was a diverse as its origins and long history of absorptions of other lines. From the largest to the smallest, each of the constituent companies had its locoshed(s) and added to the many styles of building and methods of construction.

However, generally, even in the earliest days, a form of standardisation was apparent with the timber-built broad gauge sheds of the GWR and its main associates. Whether by accident or design is not known, but most were of two straight roads, with the lines leading directly from a turntable, and had coke stages that were, more often than not, sited right outside the shed entrance.

Brick, and to a lesser extent, stone, soon supplanted timber, with its incendiary tendencies. As larger sheds became necessary, about the mid-1850s, a more or less standard pattern of straight shed was evolved. This was usually of four roads, with a single-pitched gable roof, e.g. as at Westbourne Park, Bordesley Junction, Wolverhampton, etc. It was just after this time that roundhouses were introduced — the first, at Wolverhampton, appearing in 1860. Actually 'roundhouse' is a misnomer, in as much that apart from the polygonal shed at Paddington, all of the GWR's sheds that contained a turntable were square or rectangular in plan form. The pitched roof turntable shed theme was expanded upon at Pontypool, Reading and Swindon, with double versions at Neath, Bristol and Wolverhampton, the latter being combined with the 1860 building to form a triple unit.

During his time as the GWR' CEME, William Dean standardised turntable shed design, and in the years up to 1902, a further six single-table units appeared at various points around the system; these were Cardiff (Canton), Croes Newydd, Laira, Shrewsbury, Taunton and Tondu. A common feature of the depots at Cardiff (Canton), Pontypool Road, Shrewsbury and Swindon was that the turntable sheds were directly connected internally, with straight sheds of varying sizes. Dean also gradually standardised the pattern of straight sheds, for the lesser locations, and apart from small branch line depots, oversaw the opening of nine, between the years 1882 and 1901. Following the 1877 prototype at Merthyr, Dean had, by the early 1880s, started to move away from pitched roofs for both his straight and turntable sheds, in favour of the 'northlight' or 'saw-tooth' style. This was very much in vogue on Britain's railways in the latter years of the nineteenth century but, as is well-known, the lightly constructed 'northlight' roofs were a maintenance liability, being generally unequal to the corrosion caused by the steam locomotive's by-products of soot and damp.

So, when G.J. Churchward succeeded Dean, he substituted his own design of high-pitched gable-ended roofs for both turntable and straight sheds. Seven of the former, Aberdare, Ebbw Junction, Old Oak Common, Oxley, St. Philip's Marsh, Swindon and Tyseley, and nine of the latter, Aberbeeg, Banbury, Carmarthen, Cheltenham, Fishguard, Leamington, Penzance, Severn Tunnel Junction and Westbury, were erected during Churchward's era, which saw the turntable shed reach its ultimate development on the GWR, with the massive quadruple unit at Old Oak Common — a veritable 'cathedral of steam'!

C.B. Collett saw no good reason to move away from his predecessor's designs — in most fields. Therefore, the last two turntable sheds built by the GWR, at Llanelly and Stourbridge Junction, were to Churchward's pattern, which history had proved to be excellent — for straight sheds as well. Accordingly, high-pitched gable roofs were retained for the next phase of loco

shed construction. That was during the late 1920s, early 1930s, under the auspices of the government of the day's 'Job Creation Scheme'. Known as the 'Loans and Guarantees Act' it gave money for improvements and expansion to companies like the railways, in an effort to find work for the nation's many unemployed. Apart from making considerable minor improvements, like installing electric lighting, etc., at many sheds, the GWR built, within the scheme, ten new depots between 1929 and 1934. Two-road sheds were erected at Abercynon and Kidderminster (the latter a re-erection of an earlier shed from another location), a three-road shed appeared at Shrewsbury, four-road sheds at Didcot, Laira, Landore, Pantyfynnon, Radyr and Treherbert, one eight-roader at Cardiff East Dock, and the biggest, of ten roads, was put up at Bristol (Bath Road). Construction now comprised steel frames, with corrugated asbestos for roofs and half-walls, above dwarf brick walls. The exception was the substantial ten-road depot at Bristol (Bath Road), which was built in the more traditional style of all-brick walls, with a slated roof.

One further new shed was constructed before World War II, at Aberystwyth, to be followed, after that conflict, by the final shed of all to be built by the Great Western. That was at Neath (Bridge Street), where the two-road brick and concrete shed featured a roof of unique design. Similar materials plus much glasswork were used by British Railways (Western Region), at Pwllheli, in 1958, for the very last shed to be built on the former GWR system. This method of construction differed from the only two other British Railways rebuildings, at Moat Lane and Southall, where corrugated materials were used.

Of course, in addition to all this new construction, the GWR made a number of extensions to existing sheds and carried out a considerable programme of rebuilding, of varying types and complexity. But, even so, some depots soldiered on, largely unaltered for all their existences. Notable examples were the large sheds at Gloucester, Hereford, Oxford and Worcester, each of which saw over 100 years of use. But it is among the small sheds that we find the greatest longevity, with the accolade for being the GW shed that saw the longest service to steam — 120 years — going to Brimscombe. (Brimscombe's record of continuous service has since been surpassed of course, by such places as Exeter & Machynlleth).

Despite all the expenditure mentioned above, the GWR — and British Railways (Western Region) — were very parsimonius when it came to improving one important aspect of loco shed activity. When BR rebuilt Southall in 1954, the new shed was provided with a rare facility — one of only three mechanised coaling plants to be installed at a GWR location! The others were at Worcester, where the GWR had installed a small tub and hoist system like Southall, and Birkenhead, which received a large concrete coaling tower in the mid-1950s — by default really, as it was built under a BR (Midland Region) scheme. So few mechanical coalers seems incredible when one recalls that such plants were introduced early in the twentieth century and were greatly expanded upon, during the 1920s and 1930s, by the LMS and LNER. But it must be remembered that the GWR used almost exclusively Welsh coal, the characteristics of which were said not to be compatible with the rough bulk handling of the mechanical plants. One further remembers that the Southern Railway, which also used considerable quantities of Welsh coal, and whose electrification schemes progressively diminished its steam locomotives' importance, saw fit to provide mechanical coaling plants at many of its major sheds! So, what about that coaler at Birkenhead? Presumably the GW locomotive types allocated there were using other than Welsh coals — something that traditionally was not good for them — or was it?

Mechanical coalers or no, the days of the steam locomotive came to an end and with them went the loco sheds. Today, of the over 400 sheds that ever existed on the GWR system at its greatest extent, only five remain in use by BR locomotives. The first of these is Old Oak Common, a much reduced shadow of its former self. Then comes the 115-year-old ex-Cornwall Minerals Railway building at St. Blazey, but the continued working existence of this is now in doubt — a part-roundhouse, followed by the remnants of the Cambrian depot at Machynlleth. Then, there are the two buildings at Chester, one ex-Chester & Birkenhead Railway, the other formerly LNWR. Finally, still serving BR's last steam locomotives, comes Aberystwyth. Also to be mentioned, is the 33-year-old BR building at Southall, whose existence came to an end only in Nobember 1986, as these words are being drafted. This shed is now again serving steam, as the London base of a number of privately owned steam locomotives. In addition, there are a number of former steam shed sites that are still used for stabling diesels, but where little or none of the original buildings still stand, Exeter is a notable example. However, there is another survivor, miraculously still largely complete, in the four-road standard gauge shed at Bristol (South Wales Junction), opened in 1872 and closed for locomotive use only five years later. For the remaining 110 years of its existence it has been used as a carriage shed and then a wagon shop, in which latter guise it serves today, and probably for some years yet, along with another miraculous survivor, the even older adjacent two former shed buildings of the Bristol and Gloucester Railway!

There is yet one further shed which seems destined to continue — hopefully for generations to come. That of course is the Great Western Society's working museum at Didcot. Although a relative youngster, being one of the 1930's 'Loan and Guarantees Act' buildings, this four-road depot does contain Britain's finest collection of ex-GWR locomotives, rolling stock and other memorabilia. So at Didcot, those of us who are fortunate enough to be able to remember the sheer total sensory experience of visiting a busy steam shed, can now and then recapture that feeling. At the same time, we should feel sorry for the youngsters of today, who though they may marvel at what Didcot shows them, can never *really* know, can they?

Roger Griffiths
Doha, Qatar

For Jane

ISBN 0 86093 385 7

A FOULIS—OPC Railway Book

© R. Griffiths & Haynes Publishing Group

Published by:
Haynes Publishing Group
Sparkford, Near Yeovil, Somerset BA22 7JJ

Haynes Publications Inc.
861 Lawrence Drive, Newbury Park, California 91320, USA

GWR SYSTEM MAPS

The following maps show, with a few exceptions, mainly in South Wales, the full extent of the lines of the GWR, its amalgamated companies and its joint workings. The positions of every known loco shed of every company and joint venture, are marked, even though quite a number disappeared before they came into the GWR empire. Also shown are those locations that, as far as is known, never had a shed building, but were included in one or another of the GWR's lists of locomotive sheds.

The purpose of the maps is to give an idea of just how many loco sheds existed — something over 400 — and where they were

located. If any reader wishes to investigate further, the autho wholeheartedly recommends consultation of *An Historical Survey of Great Western Engine Sheds, 1947* by E. Lyons, (OPC, 1972) and *An Historical Survey of Great Western Engine Sheds, 1837-1947 (including amalgamated companies)* by E. Lyons and E. Mountford, (OPC, 1979). Both these excellent works are a mine of information and historical detail, and the author readily acknowledges the unique assistance they rendered in the compilation of this volume.

MAP 1. LONDON, THE VALE OF THE WHITE HORSE, THE BERKS & HANTS LINE, GLOUCESTER, BIRMINGHAM & THE MIDLANDS.

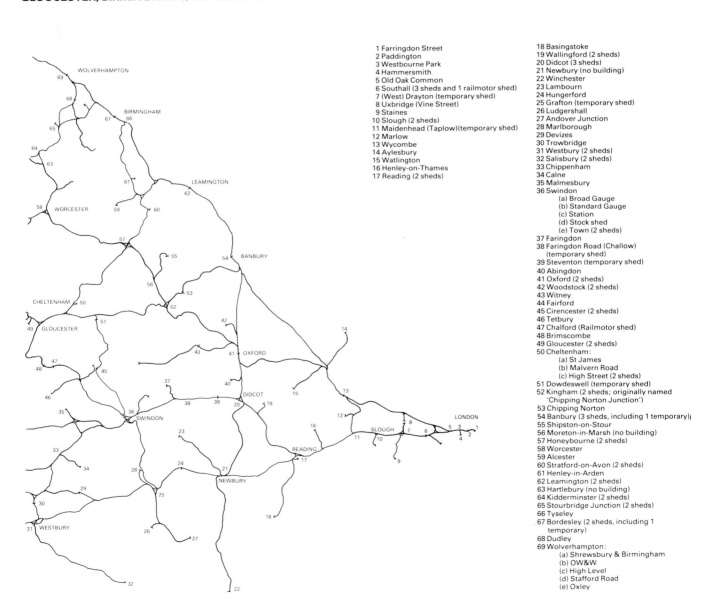

1 Farringdon Street
2 Paddington
3 Westbourne Park
4 Hammersmith
5 Old Oak Common
6 Southall (3 sheds and 1 railmotor shed)
7 (West) Drayton (temporary shed)
8 Uxbridge (Vine Street)
9 Staines
10 Slough (2 sheds)
11 Maidenhead (Taplow)(temporary shed)
12 Marlow
13 Wycombe
14 Aylesbury
15 Watlington
16 Henley-on-Thames
17 Reading (2 sheds)

18 Basingstoke
19 Wallingford (2 sheds)
20 Didcot (3 sheds)
21 Newbury (no building)
22 Winchester
23 Lambourn
24 Hungerford
25 Grafton (temporary shed)
26 Ludgershall
27 Andover Junction
28 Marlborough
29 Devizes
30 Trowbridge
31 Westbury (2 sheds)
32 Salisbury (2 sheds)
33 Chippenham
34 Calne
35 Malmesbury
36 Swindon
    (a) Broad Gauge
    (b) Standard Gauge
    (c) Station
    (d) Stock shed
    (e) Town (2 sheds)
37 Faringdon
38 Faringdon Road (Challow)
    (temporary shed)
39 Steventon (temporary shed)
40 Abingdon
41 Oxford (2 sheds)
42 Woodstock (2 sheds)
43 Witney
44 Fairford
45 Cirencester (2 sheds)
46 Tetbury
47 Chalford (Railmotor shed)
48 Brimscombe
49 Gloucester (2 sheds)
50 Cheltenham:
    (a) St James
    (b) Malvern Road
    (c) High Street (2 sheds)
51 Dowdeswell (temporary shed)
52 Kingham (2 sheds; originally named
    'Chipping Norton Junction')
53 Chipping Norton
54 Banbury (3 sheds, including 1 temporary)|
55 Shipston-on-Stour
56 Moreton-in-Marsh (no building)
57 Honeybourne (2 sheds)
58 Worcester
59 Alcester
60 Stratford-on-Avon (2 sheds)
61 Henley-in-Arden
62 Leamington (2 sheds)
63 Hartlebury (no building)
64 Kidderminster (2 sheds)
65 Stourbridge Junction (2 sheds)
66 Tyseley
67 Bordesley (2 sheds, including 1
    temporary)
68 Dudley
69 Wolverhampton:
    (a) Shrewsbury & Birmingham
    (b) OW&W
    (c) High Level
    (d) Stafford Road
    (e) Oxley

MAP 2. WEYMOUTH & THE WEST OF ENGLAND

1 Frome (2 sheds)
2 Radstock
3 Wells:
    (a) East Somerset (2 sheds)
    (b) Priory Road
    (c) Tucker Street
4 Glastonbury
5 Shepton (Mallet)
6 Yeovil (2 sheds)
7 Bridport
8 Abbotsbury
9 Weymouth (2 sheds)
10 Easton (2 sheds)
11 Chard
12 Bridgwater (2 sheds, including 1
    temporary)
13 Taunton (3 sheds)
14 Watchet
15 Minehead
16 Barnstaple
17 Wellington (Somerset)
18 Beambridge (temporary shed)
19 Burlescombe (3ft. gauge)
20 Tiverton Junction (2 sheds)
21 Hemyock
22 Stoke Canon
23 Exeter (4 sheds, including 1 temporary)
24 Ashton
25 Moretonhampstead

26 Newton Abbot (2 sheds)
27 Kingswear
28 Brixham (2 sheds)
29 Totnes
30 Ashburton
31 Kingsbridge
32 Plymouth:
    (a) Millbay
    (b) Laira
    (c) Dock
33 Princetown
34 Tavistock
35 Launceston
36 Liskeard
37 Moorswater
38 Looe
39 Bodmin
40 St Blazey
41 Stenalees
42 Burngullow
43 Newquay (2 sheds)
44 Truro (3 sheds)
45 Falmouth
46 Carn Brea
47 Helston
48 Hayle
49 St Ives
50 Penzance (3 sheds)

MAP 3. BRISTOL, THE MARCHES, NORTH, WEST & CENTRAL WALES

1 Box
2 Bath (2 sheds)
3 Bristol:
    (a) South Wales Junction
    (b) Temple Meads Station (stabling point)
    (c) Temple Meads Station (later 'Bath Road')
    (d) St Philips Marsh
    (e) Clifton (Hotwells)
4 Yatton
5 Blagdon (no building)
6 Clevedon
7 Weston-super-Mare (2 sheds)
8 Portishead
9 Avonmouth (2 sheds)
10 Shirehampton
11 Severn Tunnel Junction (2 sheds)
12 Portskewett
13 Chepstow (2 sheds, including 1 temporary)
14 Lydney
15 Bullo Pill
16 Hopebrook (temporary shed)
17 Ross-on-Wye
18 Hereford (2 sheds)
19 Pontrilas (2 sheds)
20 Clifford
21 Malvern Wells (2 sheds)
22 Ledbury (no building)
23 Bromyard
24 Leominster (2 sheds)
25 Kington
26 Woofferton
27 Ludlow
28 Clee Hill
29 Cleobury Town (2 sheds)
30 Much Wenlock
31 Wellington
32 Market Drayton
33 Crewe (Gresty Lane)
34 Shrewsbury:
    (a) Abbey Foregate (S&BR)
    (b) Coleham (S&HR) (later GW/LNW Joint)
    (c) Coton Hill (GWR)
    (d) Coton Hill (S&CR)
35 Oswestry
36 Gobowen
37 Whitchurch (LNWR shed)
38 Trevor (Pontcysyllte)
39 Ruabon
40 Croes Newydd
41 Wrexham Central
42 Summerhill
43 Brymbo
44 Saltney
45 Chester
46 Hooton
47 Birkenhead (2 sheds)
48 Corwen
49 Bala
50 Trawsfynydd

51 Tranymanod (also known as 'Manod')
52 Portmadoc (2 sheds)
53 Pwllheli (3 sheds)
54 Penmaenpool
55 Llangynog
56 Llanfyllin
57 Welshpool (2 sheds including one 2ft. 6in. gauge)
58 Kerry
59 Moat Lane (2 sheds)
60 Caersws
61 Dinas Mawddwy (2 sheds)
62 Corris (Maespoeth)
63 Machynlleth
64 Aberystwyth (3 sheds, including one 1ft. 11½in. gauge.)
65 Llanidloes (3 sheds)
66 Builth Wells
67 Aberayron (2 sheds)
68 Newcastle Emlyn
69 Pencader
70 Llandovery
71 Brecon (3 sheds)
72 Talyllyn Junction
73 Talybont
74 Garnant (2 sheds)
75 Mountain (Tirydail)
76 Pantyfynnon
77 Landore

78 Swansea:
    (a) Burrows Lodge
    (b) Danygraig
    (c) East Dock
    (d) Harbour
    (e) High Street
    (f) Prince of Wales
    (g) Riverside (Rowland)
    (h) Riverside (R&SB)
    (i) Riverside (VoN)
    (j) Riverside (Westlake) (2 sheds)
    (k) St. Thomas
79 Llanelly:
    (a) Sandy (Pwll) (2 sheds)
    (b) Dock (2 sheds)
    (c) GWR
80 Burry Port
81 Kidwelly
82 Carmarthen:
    (a) C&CR (2 sheds)
    (b) Junction (2 sheds)
    (c) GWR
83 Whitland (2 sheds)
84 Llanfalteg
85 Cardigan
86 Tenby (3 sheds)
87 Pembroke Dock
88 Milford Haven (2 sheds)

89 Neyland
90 Rosebush (2 sheds)
91 Letterston (2 sheds)
92 Goodwick

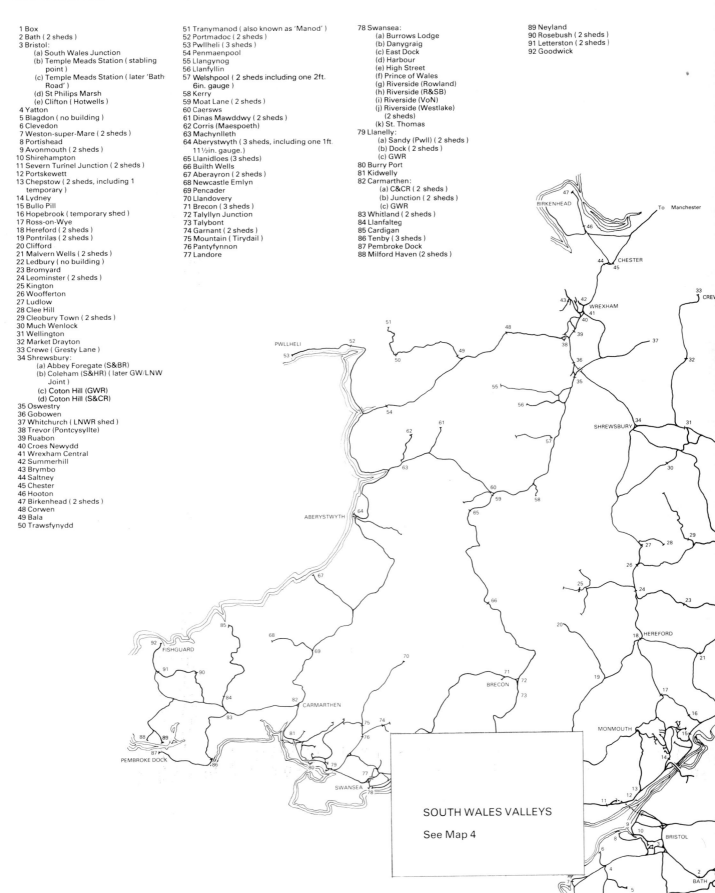

SOUTH WALES VALLEYS

See Map 4

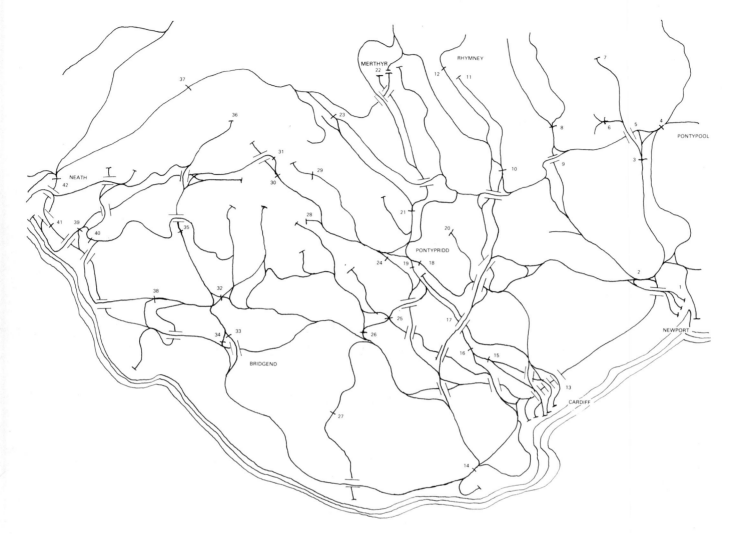

MAP 4. SOUTH WALES VALLEYS (layout simplified)

1 Newport:
   (a) Bolt Street
   (b) Court y Bella
   (c) Dock
   (d) Dock Street
   (e) Ebbw Junction
   (f) High Street
   (g) Pill (also called West
      Mendalgief)
2 Bassaleg
3 Pontypool (Coed y Grig)
4 Pontypool Road
5 Pontypool, Crane Street
6 Branches Fork
7 Blaenavon
8 Aberbeeg (2 sheds)
9 Crumlin
10 Fleur-de-Lis
11 Pontllotyn
12 Rhymney

13 Cardiff:
   (a) Bute Yard (Tyndall Street)
   (b) Canton
   (c) Cathays
   (d) Crwys Yard
   (e) Docks (also called 'Parade')
   (f) East Dock
   (g) East Moors
   (h) Newtown
   (i) Penarth Dock
   (j) Penarth Town
   (k) Terminus (TVR) (2 sheds)
   (l) West Yard
14 Barry (2 sheds plus 1 railmotor shed)
15 Roath Branch Junction
16 Radyr (2 sheds)
17 Taff Wells (Walnut Tree Jct)
18 Glyntaff (Pontypridd) (2 sheds
   including 1 railmotor shed)

19 Coke Ovens (Pontypridd) (2 sheds
   including 1 railmotor shed)
20 Sengenhydd
21 Abercynon (2 sheds)
22 Dowlais/Merthyr:
   (a) Cae Harris
   (b) Dowlais Central (2 sheds)
   (c) Ivor Junction
   (d) Pant
   (e) Merthyr High Street (2 sheds)
   (f) Merthyr (TVR) (2 sheds)
23 Aberdare:
   (a) Aberdare Railway (2 sheds)
   (b) GWR/Vale of Neath
   (c) GWR (2 sheds)
   (d) TVR
24 Trehafod (Hafod)
25 Common Branch Junction
26 Llantrisant (2 sheds)
27 Cowbridge (2 sheds)

28 Pwllyrhebog (2 sheds)
29 Ferndale (2 sheds)
30 Treherbert (2 sheds)
31 Blaenrhondda (2 sheds)
32 Tondu (3 sheds)
33 Coity Junction
34 Bridgend
35 Maesteg
36 Glyncorrwg
37 Glyn Neath
38 Penylan
39 Duffryn Yard
40 Aberavon
41 Briton Ferry (2 sheds)
42 Neath:
   (a) Vale of Neath (2 sheds including 1
      temporary)
   (b) Court Sart
   (c) Bridge Street (2 sheds)

THE SHEDS

Author's Note: The format of this book differs slightly from the two previous volumes in the series, which covered the sheds of the LMS and LNER. Those books featured separate sections for servicing facilities — coalers, turntables, etc. — and, at the end, the fate of some sheds, after closure to steam. *GWR Sheds in Camera* simply features sheds in alphabetical order and, where appropriate, includes servicing facilities, breakdown trains, sheds closed and in other use, etc. In addition, a few depots are covered in depth, by a series of pictures, in special 'Focus' sections.

However, there the differences end, because just like John Hooper, who so ably compiled the LMS and LNER books, the author set out to use as much previously unpublished — and non-official — material as possible, and to restrict pictures featuring diesels to an absolute minimum (GWR diesel railcars are acceptable — just!). Needless to say, those requirements have not been entirely met, but the author hopes that the following 308 photographs, covering 164 different sheds, will give satisfaction nevertheless.

Plate 2: The Abbotsbury Railway, from Upwey Junction to Abbotsbury, was absorbed by the GWR in 1896. The little stone-built shed, opened with the line on 9th November 1885, was immediately closed by its new owners, who removed the roof and left the rest to moulder. The sad but defiant remains are seen here, during the severe winter of early 1963, no less than 67 years after closure. The structure in the foreground had supported a water tank and stood opposite a coaling platform.

C. L. Caddy

Plate 3: The GWR completed its Aberayon branch as late as 1911, from a junction north of Lampeter, on the former Manchester & Milford Railway's Aberystwyth to Carmarthen line. The branch terminus was provided with a single-road wooden shed, which housed a normal allocation of one or two tank locomotives. The shed burned down in 1925, so in the following year, the GWR dismantled the redundant ex-Cambrian Railways shed at Wrexham (Central), and re-erected it at Aberayron. That corrugated structure is seen on 19th September 1962, five months after official closure, although, by the look of it, the shed had not been used for some time before that.

W. T. Stubbs Collection

Plate 4: The last of nine Churchward standard straight sheds to be erected, a four-road building scaling 210ft. × 66ft. for twelve tender, or twenty tank locomotives, was provided at Aberbeeg, opening on 7th April 1919. It replaced the 61-year-old ex-Monmouthshire Railway & Canal Company's shed, which stood a few hundred yards to the north, and had for a long time been inadequate for its allocation of about a dozen engines. The author well remembers calling at Aberbeeg on numerous occasions, from the 1950s. This was always early on a Sunday morning, as the first visit of an overnight 'shed bash' from London. One memory that remains is of a shed full of silent locomotives, inevitably outnumbered by not nearly so silent half-wild sheep! This very pleasant view, with an 0-6-0PT officiating on coal stage pilot duties, was taken on 16th August 1953.

B. Hilton

Plate 5: The more usual viewpoint for photographing Aberbeeg Shed. It is here seen in June 1977, following private purchase some years before and conversion into an iron foundry.

Author

Plate 6: The Taff Vale Railway opened a one-engine shed at Abercynon, then known as Aberdare Junction, in 1853. This building must soon have been totally inadequate, and by 1926 the allocation had grown to 19 locomotives. Replacement finally occurred in 1929, with a two-road corrugated structure, which basically formed the prototype for the numerous 'Loans and Guarantees Act' sheds that were to be built over the next five years. The shed is depicted on 25th August 1935, with a typical line-up of GWR and constituent companies engines — note the commendable cleanliness. Closure came in November 1962, but the building still stands, in use by an engineering company.

B. Matthews

Plate 7: The Churchward single turntable shed at Aberdare, on 25th August 1935, with the repair shop prominent on the left. This shed was the seventh to be sited at Aberdare, to service the engines moving trains of coal from the Dare and Cynon valleys. First, were the two short-lived sheds of the Aberdare Railway, which were followed in 1864 by the Vale of Neath Railway's shed, when that line arrived 'over the hill' from Neath. The Taff Vale Railway's depot was next, opening in 1865, and eventually comprising two buildings — that closed in 1927. The GWR built a four-road shed in 1867, adjacent to its by then joint premises with the VoNR. Booming traffic caused the four-road shed to be doubled in width only seven years later, the GWR/VoNR joint shed closing, meanwhile. The last shed, depicted here, opened on 11th November 1907, replacing the eight-road shed. Final closure was at the beginning of March 1965.

B. Matthews

Plate 8: The wisdom of Churchward's opting for high-pitched gable roofs for his sheds is amply demonstrated by the light and airy interior of Aberdare. Note the 65ft. manual turntable with open pit. All the engines on view, on 13th July 1958, are 'at home', except for Pontypool Road's No. 7724, which had worked across on the line via Crumlin and Quakers Yard.

H. C. Casserley

Plates 9 & 10: The Cambrian Railway opened its first shed at Aberystwyth in June 1864, the building becoming joint premises when the grandiosely-named Manchester & Milford Railway arrived three years later. The M&MR's hopeless aspirations ended in 1906 when the GWR took over the company and continued the joint arrangements. The shed was deemed life-expired by 1938, so the GWR replaced it with a very similar structure on the same site, but with working improvements for the men and machines employed there. The upper view shows the first shed, from the station, on 7th January 1937. At one time an elevated water tank had stood just to the right of the camera, with a turntable between it and the shed. However, in 1925, the station was extended, so the tank and turntable had to be moved. The former was placed atop a new coal stage, while the turntable's new location can just be made out, to the right of the sand house. The hoist was retained when the Great Western built the 1938 shed, which is visible below, in a busy scene in early April 1959. From left to right are Moguls No. 6329 of Carmarthen, having just worked up from there, Tyseley's No. 5369, waiting to return with its train from Birmingham, and No. 6371, a Machynlleth engine, which with the unidentified Class 2251 0-6-0 alongside, was 'brewing up' in readiness, possibly, to back down on to the two rakes of coaches visible at the station platforms.

BR/OPC & K. Fairey

Plates 11 & 12: Aberystwyth's other railway, the Vale of Rheidol Light, opened for business in 1902. The shed comprised two adjoining buildings, with a water tank; coaling was done from wagons. This charming installation is seen above, with No. 9 in residence on 3rd August 1955, which must have been a hot and dreamy day, to judge by the locoman taking his ease in the grass! Such an idyll did not last, however, as in 1968, the VoR's operations were transferred, in their entirety, to the standard gauge shed. The August 1978 picture below shows this, converted for narrow gauge use. With the exception of the watering arrangements, nearly all the standard gauge facilities have disappeared. The crane's retention is almost certainly why the coal stage and water tank have survived, but the latter's 45,000 gallon capacity could perhaps be described as lavish! Nevertheless, this was the very last in a line of over 400 working steam sheds that served the GWR and its constituents until joined very recently by Southall. Long may both continue to serve the cause of steam!

W. Potter & J. Peden

Plate 13: Two sheds for the price of one photograph! Andover Junction on 17th May 1953, with the ex-LSWR shed on the left, and the wooden ex-GWR shed on the right, with No. 6357 on view. The GWR building had a complex history. Built in 1883 by the LSWR, it was rented to the Swindon, Marlborough & Andover Railway, to later come under the auspices of the Midland & South Western Junction Railway, and GWR, respectively. The LSWR shed, alongside, opened in 1904, with both companies having separate coaling facilities but sharing the turntable which was sited between and behind the two buildings. Amazingly, BR(Western and Southern regions) perpetuated the separate coaling arrangements, with the former using the canopied coal stage installed by the GWR about 1935: this had replaced the stone-built SMAR coaling platform visible between the two buildings. Closure of the GWR shed came in 1958, while the LSWR depot lasted until June 1962.

T. J. Edgington

Plate 14: Ashburton was the last shed to be built by the South Devon Railway, for a lease company, the Buckfastleigh, Totnes & South Devon Railway. It opened in 1872 and was absorbed in 1897 by the GWR, who made no changes, preferring instead to close the shed at Totnes, the main line junction, in 1904. Officially, Ashburton closed on 10th September 1962, but this photograph, taken a year before that, shows the building already converted for other use. After the Dart Valley Railway Preservation Society's failure to retain the Buckfastleigh to Ashburton section of the line, the extended building was taken over by a commercial concern.

W. T. Stubbs Collection

Plate 15: The Teign Valley Railway reached Ashton, from Heathfield, in 1882, and opened its only shed at the terminus. Thus it remained until the line was extended to Exeter, in 1903, whereupon the shed's usefulness declined and closure came around 1908. In a view taken circa 1910, looking south from the station, the rear of the shed is visible, with the prominent water tank having a lean-to pumping house. The dark-coloured structure between the tank and the shed was the canopied coal platform.

Author's Collection

Plate 16: The GWR gained a loco shed at Aylesbury through the company's working of the Aylesbury & Buckingham Railway, from 1863. That line eventually became a satellite of the Metropolitan Railway, but the GWR continued using the shed, for the locomotives working the Princes Risborough branch. However, there was indecision as to Aylesbury's status, because while classifying it a sub-shed of Slough, locomotives were supplied from Paddington (Old Oak Common) and Banbury! After nationalisation, the shed became subsidiary to the ex-LNER depot at Neasden, and it is one of that shed's ex-LMS 2-6-4 tanks that is seen on 31st March 1960. All the surviving facilities are on view, the turntable initially provided having lasted only a few years. The coal platform's cast-iron canopy once supported a water tank — the BR-installed replacement is visible beyond. The advent of diesels caused the depot's closure in June 1962.

BR/OPC

Plate 17: Built by the Bala & Festiniog Railway, the little depot at Bala opened in 1882. Of classic branch line shed appearance, it had a water tank on the roof, hand-coaling from wagons, and covered accommodation for, at most, two tank engines. Seen here in a distant view, on 15th June 1958, 0-6-0PT No. 4645 is shunting wagons under the GW-installed coaling canopy; Nos. 7440, 8791 and 9669 were also present that day. Another GWR addition was a brick-built locomen's room at the rear of the shed, while a 50ft. turntable, sited behind the camera, completed the facilities. The line and shed were casualties of the 'Beeching Plan' and closure came in January 1965.

B. Hilton

Plate 18: An all too familiar scene, from the mid-late 1960s, after 'Beeching's Butchers' had been and gone. The remains of Bala Shed slowly rot away, on 2nd August 1969, waiting for someone to come along and finish the job. Meanwhile, 'Mother Nature' does what she can to soften the vandals' scars.

H. Stevenson

Plates 19 & 20: Banbury's 1908 Churchward shed (above), on 7th May 1961, still staunchly Great Western in content, with the tender of No. 6926 *Holkham Hall* showing signs of only partly effective treatment by the cleaners. But, in 1963, the Midland Region took over and GWR locomotive classes began their steady decline. So did standards decline, and after two years of Midland Region control (below) locomotive cleanliness left a lot to be desired! Yet, though shorn of her nameplates and smokebox numberplate, No. 6993, formerly *Arthog Hall*, maintains a grimy dignity as she awaits her imminent fate. Banbury Shed was an important and busy depot for most of its life, particularly during the two world wars. This is evidenced by the 1944 extension to the coaling stage, done in an effort to increase the through-put of locomotives — including many USATC 2-8-0s — working the dense wartime traffic through this major centre. Nevertheless, in time, traffic declined, and Banbury Shed closed on 3rd October 1966.

K. Fairey

Plate 21: An air of rural calm pervades as 'Bulldog' No. 3430 *Inchcape* slumbers beside the one-time broad gauge shed at Barnstaple (GW), circa 1936. Built by the Devon & Somerset Railway, a lease company of the B&ER, the shed was opened in 1873. The complete depot is seen — coal platform, turntable, pits, etc., all little changed during the shed's 78-year life. The track branching off to the right, behind the shed, is a connection to the LSWR's line, a signal controlling which is visible between *Inchcape* and the coal platform.

B. Matthews

Plates 22 & 23: Two views of the south end of the main shed of the erstwhile Barry Railway. The above dates from about 1930, and must have been taken on a Sunday, because of the large number of locomotives on shed, and mostly out of steam — at least 55 may be counted. Soon the firelighters would descend on the depot and a pall of smoke would gather, as the engines were readied for Monday's return to work. Below, from the coal stage, on the last day of August 1947, several ex-Barry Railway locomotives were still to be seen. Giving a lift to an 0-6-2T was an ex-Barry Railway steam crane, a Cowans Sheldon product, with a 25 ton capacity (15 ton with a 20ft. jib), supplied in 1919. Numbered 14 in the GWR's crane list, it had moved to Margam by 1961 and was part of the Chief Civil Engineer's stock at Radyr, in 1970, after which all trace was lost.

W. H. Whitworth & W. Potter

Plate 24: The other end of Barry's 'northlight'-roofed shed on 26th July 1953, with a visiting LNWR 0-8-0 stealing the scene. These engines were regular visitors from Tredegar Depot on summer Sunday excursions from the Sirhowy Valley (Brynmawer and Pontllanfraith). Notice the target on No. 6641's lamp bracket — 'BG' meaning the locomotive is engaged on local passenger duties. The shed was closed to steam during May 1964 and survives today, in use as a wagon repair depot.

L. B. Lapper courtesy N. E. Preedy

Plate 25: The fitting shed at Barry, sited at the south-west corner of the shed yard. The author has heard a rumour, as yet unconfirmed, that this building was constructed from materials recovered from the Barry Railway's very first shed. That was a former contractor's depot which stood on the site of the later Works and closed when the permanent shed opened in 1890. Anyhow, by August 1947, above, the shear legs, formerly positioned outside the fitting shed, had been removed, and the building was mostly used for the storage and stabling of engines. The doyen of the GWR's Class 5600 0-6-2T is seen heading a line of ex-Barry Railway locomotives — two Class B1 and one Class B.

W. Potter

Plate 26: The Great Western shed at Basingstoke, a sub-depot of Reading, around the time of nationalisation, giving shelter to nought but a couple of the staff's bicycles! Of brick and wood construction, the shed's decidedly unkempt appearance should be no surprise as it was approaching its one hundredth birthday — a venerable survivor from the days of the broad gauge. This might be due to the fact that it seems never to have been a particularly busy depot, and one whose importance declined steadily with the years. An allocation of one 0-6-0T, one 2-6-2T, and a pair of Moguls, in 1921, had declined to three 0-6-0 pannier tanks by nationalisation. Closure came nearly three years later, in November 1950.

Author's Collection

Plate 27: An undated, less than sharp picture, but important nonetheless, as it shows the elusive second Brecon & Merthyr Railway shed at Bassaleg, opened in 1921. This 200ft. × 30ft. corrugated-iron structure, which was built to share the allocation of the B&M's overtaxed 1875 building, served only eight years before being closed. However, three years later, in 1932, it was re-erected at Kidderminster, under the 'Loans and Guarantees Act' scheme. There it served for a further thirty two years *(see Plate 116).*

W. R. Dyer Collection

Plate 28: The small GWR shed at Bath, on the evening of 29th March 1959. Basically a water tank with space beneath, the original timber cladding had been replaced but little else has changed since opening nearly 79 years before — except the tenants, of course! Closure was 23 months away, leaving the one-time Roman city of Aquae Sulis without a Great Western engine shed again, for the first time in 121 years.

T. W. Nicholls

Plate 29: The Great Western 'side' of the twin eight-road GWR/LNWR shed at Birkenhead, with decidedly un-Great Western occupants! The date is May 1955 and work was in progress by BR (Midland Region) to provide a mechanised coaling plant, replacing the hitherto separate arrangements; this work has caused the loss of one shed road, as can be seen on the left. Despite the lack of GWR locomotives on view, there were still some 40 allocated at this time, but all had gone by 1963, by which time the shed had been re-roofed. Closure to steam was in November 1965, and completely, on 24th November 1985.

J. Peden

Plate 30: 'Metro' tank No. 3575 stands on the GWR 45ft. turntable at Birkenhead, in July 1937.

W. Potter

Plate 31: A view from the platform end, of Bodmin loco shed. Opened in 1887, the depot was to see some changes after this 1935 picture was taken. The tank on the rear of the roof would be removed and replaced by a GWR conical top parachute tank, outside the shed entrance, and the wooden coal platform would be superseded by a brick-built version. The shed closed in April 1962, but was subsequently used for some years by the South-West Branch of the Great Western Society.

B. Matthews

Plate 32: Welsh idyll! Three enthusiasts (does the reader recognise anyone?), from the late 1940s, probably, stand in front of the little-known depot of Branches Fork. Opened in 1892 and situated on a spur off the Pontypool to Blaenavon line, near Pontnewynydd, the shed provided engines for working two mineral lines — the Cwmnantddu branch and the Cwmffrwdder branch. No doubt much to the relief of many a non-Welsh wagon despatcher, those branches, and the shed, closed at the beginning of 1952. The usual allocation was two or three 0-6-0T.

B. Matthews Collection

Plate 33: The 73-year-old ex-Brecon & Merthyr wooden shed at Brecon, with a collection of 0-6-0s, on a Sunday in August 1936. LMS locomotives were a regular feature, having worked in from either of the two ex-MR outposts of Hereford or Swansea. Bill Camwell took this picture from the coal stage, on the other side of which, until 1934, had stood a Cambrian Railways shed, which closed in 1922. One other shed should be mentioned, the Neath & Brecon Railway's depot, which stood by that company's first station from 1867 to 1875. The B&MR shed closed in its 99th year and, from all that railway history, Brecon today shares, with a number of other places, the dubious distinction of being a (former) county town without a railway of any sort.

W. A. Camwell

Plates 34 & 35: The Bristol & Exeter Railway reached Bridgwater in mid-1841, and for a year, had a two-road temporary loco shed there. Later, the GWR erected a carriage and wagon works at Bridgwater, incorporating an engine shed in the main building. The photograph above, admittedly of poor quality, is included because of its (so far) uniqueness. It shows the shed on 10th June 1935, in original condition, although some re-roofing is evident in the adjoining bay of the wagon works. Apart from the works pilot, this shed housed an unusual locomotive in its latter years — ex-Cardiff Railway 0-4-0ST No. 1338, used in Bridgwater Docks. The Works was progressively altered and eventually the loco shed stood alone. The remains, in the depressing surroundings of a car scrapyard, are seen below, late in 1975, thirteen years after closure. J. F. Ritchie, landscape gardener and nurserieman (*sic*), could use a lesson or two in signwriting and spelling it seems.

B. Matthews & Author

Plate 36: The Bridport Railway opened on 7th November 1857 and had its workings taken over by the GWR in 1882, with complete absorption from 1st July 1901. The stone-built loco shed survived all this and was closed at the ripe old age of 102, but branch services continued for some years after. Seen here in 1963, the shed seems to be in casual use still, although the GWR-pattern gantry coaler (usually clad in corrugated material) looks a mite rusty. The only other GWR influence is the charming little ivied wooden office, still with stern admonition to would-be trespassers!

C. L. Caddy

Plate 37: Longest-lived of all Great Western sheds in the service of steam Brimscombe, functioned for no less than 120 years. Seen here on 12th September 1964, six months before final closure, the original broad gauge section is at the rear, while the ornate stone edifice, with 20,000 gallon water tank atop, was a later (date unknown) extension. Use of a Mogul on banking duties to Sapperton Summit should not be considered remarkable in the disordered last days of steam. However, a few years before, such a locomotive would have been extraordinary indeed! Various broad and standard gauge 0-6-0s — usually tanks — monopolised the depot's duties from 1845 to 1907. In that year, 2-6-2Ts of Classes 3100 and 3150 appeared, to start an association that would last for 50 years — one engine in particular, No. 3171, serving continuously from January 1930 until withdrawal, in July 1957. After the 3150s, various other Large Prairie classes were used, until the shed officially closed on 28th October 1963. Nevertheless, it remained available for stabling bankers sent from Gloucester on a day-to-day basis. Demolished following final closure, traces of one side wall remain today, over 140 years since the first brick was laid.

W. Potter

Plates 38 & 39: Bristol (Bath Road), before and after the rebuilding programme of 1932-4. Above, in 1926, is the entrance to the double turntable shed, converted in 1877 from the B&ER's Works. Out of view, to the left, stood a six-road straight shed, the original B&ER broad gauge depot, later adapted for standard gauge use. Both buildings were progressively razed from 1932 and replaced by the shed below, seen on 12th June 1949, with a marvellous panorama of power. The new depot was the ultimate 'Loans Act' shed, with ten roads, all the usual offices, messrooms and stores, a large coaler with 135,000 gallon tank, two turntables — one in the yard and the other at the back of the depot — and a spacious workshop. However, it was destined to serve only for 26 years, being closed in September 1960 for rebuilding, yet again, into a diesel depot. As such it survives today, including the large workshop and rear turntable.

B. J. Miller & N. E. Preedy

Plate 40: A typical view from Bristol (Temple Meads) Station platforms, looking towards Bristol (Bath Road) depot yard. The epitome of grace and symmetry, two generations of Great Western four-cylinder 4-6-0 pose for the cameraman on 6th August 1955. One of the last 'Stars', No. 4056 *Princess Margaret* (complete with slightly bent bufferbeam) and 'Castle' No. 5000 *Launceston Castle*, were both among Bath Road's allocation of about 95 engines at that time.

W. Potter

Plate 41: Just visible in the two preceding pictures, and here seen in close-up — the self-propelled steam grab crane used for clearing Bath Road's ash pits. Such machines were seen at the GWR's larger sheds, being numbered in the railway's list of cranes, but nothing can be discerned about this particular example, sad to say. The date too is unknown but was probably close to the end of the GWR's existence.

Woodfin Collection, Courtesy of Bristol City Museum

Plate 42: Opened in July 1910 to relieve the burdens being placed on nearby Bath Road Depot, the Churchward double turntable shed at Bristol (St. Philip's Marsh) is here seen at the moment of closure, in June 1964. It predominantly housed goods engines all its life, until the last four years, when it took over such steam passenger duties as remained after Bristol (Bath Road) closed for rebuilding. On its own closure, the locomotives remaining at SPM (one of its GWR codings) moved to the 91-year-old ex-MR turntable shed at Bristol (Barrow Road). Steam lingered there until Barrow Road succumbed in October 1965, and closed the book on the city of Bristol's 125 years of steam locomotives and their sheds.

A. G. Ellis Collection

Plate 43: The interior of St. Philip's Marsh Shed, a month before closure, featuring some intricate roofing and smoke vent detail. Officially withdrawn in February 1964, No. 2247 was, it seems, still in use, although the notice chalked on her cabside probably indicates her imminent departure to the Bridgend yard of R. S. Hayes Ltd., where she met her fate.

D. K. Jones

Plate 44: One of the privileges of being a Bristol railwayman! St. Philip's Marsh, 8th May 1964, when Terry Nicholls just happened to be around when three members of the rapidly dwindling 'Castle' class just happened to be on shed at the same time! No. 5054 *Earl of Ducie* faces her double-chimneyed sister, No. 7003 *Elmley Castle* (both former Bath Road engines), across the turntable, while No. 4077 *Chepstow Castle* watches through the doorway. Next day, the never-to-be-forgotten 9th May 1964, was the 60th anniversary of *City of Truro's* epic flight. *Earl of Ducie* whisked the commemorative Great Western Railtour, with the author among the spellbound passengers, from Bristol to Paddington in just over 95 minutes. If ever there was a cry to be spared from the cutter's torch! But, *Clun Castle's* record performance on the Plymouth to Bristol leg of the railtour ensured that she would survive, while No. 5054 died, only five months later, in Swindon's 'C' Shop. Chalked on her remains was her epitaph, from a driver at Worcester, her last shed. It said:

Goodbye mate you've done your best,
Come on inside and have a rest,
To scrap this 'Earl' is such a shame,
As this old girl isn't really lame.

T. W. Nicholls

Plate 45: An incredible survivor! The former standard gauge shed at Bristol (South Wales Junction). Opened in 1872, it served locomotives for just five years, before conversion to a wagon shop, and is still in use today! It is seen here, from the rear, in June 1978, with the original doors and wooden roof gable still intact. The GWR's first Bristol shed, a three-road broad gauge building, once stood to the left of this scene. Out of picture, to the right, are the still extant two-road and three-road former loco shed buildings of the Bristol & Gloucester Railway. These date back to the early 1840s, and are also in use as wagon shops.

Author

Plate 46: The Cambrian Railway erected a shed in the small Welsh spa town of Builth Wells in 1864. Serving for 93 years until closure in September 1957, it is depicted here on 15th September 1949, with 'Dean Goods' No. 2452 finding itself hemmed-in by a 20 ton brake van. Note the neatly buttressed dwarf brick walls and the corrugated upper walls and roof. The latter is almost certainly a GWR modification, the shed formerly having a higher pitched gable, as at Aberayron. (*Plate 3*).

T. J. Edgington

Plate 47: Typical of the numerous Welsh railway companies, the Burry Port & Gwendraeth Valley Railway flourished from opening in 1875, and is still open for traffic — no mean feat, considering today's much-pruned railway network. The company's depot was at Burry Port, a three-road brick and wood building, seen here in April 1949, with ex-BPGV 0-6-0T No. 2167 and Class 1901 0-6-0PT No. 2019 taking in the sunshine. The ash of many years service lies in the foreground while we are left to ponder upon the purpose of the partly-interred oil drums!

W. Potter

Plate 48: A quarter of a century has passed, steam locomotives have been gone for 12 years, and Burry Port depot serves in the inglorious role of a garage for the all-conquering heavy lorry. Mercifully, the building has since been demolished.

Author

Plate 49: The spoil tips of many decades of mining form a backdrop to Cae Harris Depot, the usually wet and windy GWR/Rhymney Railway outpost at Dowlais. Early in BR days, the shed is seen with some work being done to the ashpit on one of the roads. The coaling platform is on the left, and the wagons to the right stand on the access road to a seldom-used turntable at the rear of the shed. In the foreground a lone enthusiast consults his notebook and laments, probably, at finding only No. 5671 and one of her sisters in occupancy. Let us hope he 'copped' them both!

B. Matthews Collection

Plate 50: On 13th June 1964, typical Cae Harris weather greets another band of pilgrims, come to worship on the last day of passenger services between Dowlais and Nelson & Llancaiach. BR has provided a gantry coaling plant, but to little avail, as the shed and its Class 5600 locomotives were to disappear forever from Dowlais only six months after this picture was taken. The 'KO SPECIAL' target was carried by the enthusiasts' special train.

W. Potter

Plate 51: Cardiff was rich in railway history, with four different companies having no fewer than eleven sheds between them over the years. The smallest company was the Cardiff Railway, renamed in 1897 from the Bute Dock Company, which itself had previously been the Marquess of Bute Railways, until 1887. The MoBR's first shed had opened in 1862, at Bute Yard — or Tyndall Street as it was also known. This two-road stone-built shed closed in 1891 when East Moors Depot opened, but survived, for many years, in works use. It is seen here in 1926, serving, among other things, as a chain shop. Note the period motor car.

BR/OPC

Plate 52: Cardiff (Canton) was the GWR's main shed at Cardiff, from 1882, until closure for rebuilding as a diesel depot, in September 1962. This gloriously grimy elevated shot shows the eastern end of the shed in mid-August 1951, with a 'Castle' bearing the famous Canton 'supershine' prominent on the right. The footbridge passes in front of the original six-road straight shed (the first large Dean 'northlight' building) later re-roofed by BR, while the 1897 turntable shed at the rear is obscured by all that delicious pollution! Just above the footbridge, on the left, can be seen a wartime ash shelter, with line-up of locomotives from the coaling stage, which is hidden by the repair shops to the right of the ash shelter.

S. C. L. Phillips (D. K. Jones Collection)

Plate 53: The western edifice of Cardiff (Canton) on 6th July 1952, with reboilered ex-TVR Class A 0-6-2T, Nos 381, 335 and 349, and 0-6-0PT No. 9713 intruding. Through the 'northlight-roofed turntable shed the eastern entrance can be seen, and beyond that the south wall of the straight shed.

W. Potter

Plate 54: Cardiff (Canton) was unusual in having a Mundt-type turntable — i.e. one that required no balancing, as the engine weight was borne by the ends. This had been installed in 1931, replacing a standard GWR over-girder type at the other end of the shed. Here the 60ft. 'Mundt' table turns BR Standard No. 75007, on 20th September 1955, while No. 6985 *Parwick Hall* waits its turn, and a Class 9400 0-6-0PT shunts the coal yard.

B. K. B. Green

Plate 55: The Taff Vale Railway had three sheds in the Cardiff Docks area between the years 1845 and 1884, when the company commissioned a spacious ten-road depot at Cathays. That shed, with its two distinctive pitched roofs, is seen on 25th August 1935, with one Class 5600 0-6-2T and various ex-TVR locomotives scattered around.

B. Matthews

Plate 56: During 1937/8, Cardiff (Cathays) lost one of its five-road bays, leaving only a repair shop at the rear. Sometime around the mid-1950s, the reduced building is seen with a solitary ex-TVR tank and numerous GWR 0-6-2T and 2-6-2T engines basking in the evening sunshine, before resuming their duties on the Cardiff Valleys suburban services — soon to be dieselised. Cathays closed to steam in 1961.

B. Matthews Collection

Plate 57: Class 5600 0-6-2T No. 5652 receives attention under the hoist in Cardiff (Cathays) gas-lit repair shop, on 23rd July 1957. This repair facility still exists and found fame in 1985, when its artisans built some replica broad gauge rolling stock, to accompany the replica Gooch 4-2-2 *Iron Duke* at the 'GW150' celebrations.

K. Fairey

Plate 58: A superb aerial view of Cardiff Docks, showing, just right of centre, the eight-road 'Loans Act' shed of Cardiff East Dock. It stands on the site of the former Rhymney Railway's four-road loco shed and Works, opened in October 1857. The Works's fitting and carriage shops were both converted into three-road loco sheds in 1901, until the whole installation progressively disappeared to make way for the new 'Loans Act' shed. Near the bottom centre of the picture are two long buildings with ventilators on their roofs — these just about mark the site of the Cardiff Railway shed of East Moors, mentioned in the caption to *Plate 51*. East Moors closed in early March 1926.

B. Hilton Collection

Plate 59: The 1931 shed at Cardiff East Dock seems to have been something of a white elephant for part of its life, its eight roads hardly being justified by the number of engines working there. In fact, actual abandonment did occur, between March 1958 and September 1962 when, with the closure of Cardiff (Canton), East Dock reopened to 'superstar' status, with most of Canton's locomotives and workings transferred there. This picture was taken in the month of reopening, when 68 locomotives were allocated, including nine 'Castles', nineteen 'Halls', three 'Granges' and two 'Manors'. This glorious era lasted until closure in August 1965.

W. T. Stubbs Collection

Plate 60: The GWR had a history of three sheds at Carmarthen. The first two were taken over from other companies; the Carmarthen & Cardigan Railway's two-road shed from 1881, until it was sold to the LNWR in April 1897, and the South Wales Railway's broad gauge shed, absorbed in 1862 and closed on 11th February 1907. On that date the shed seen here was opened — a Churchward six-road depot, with a repair shop visible on the left. Carmarthen's Nos 6347 and 7825 *Lechlade Manor* pose for the photographer in June 1958, just under six years before closure.

W. Potter

Plate 61: Main depot of the Hayle Railway, Carn Brea was an early shed, opening in 1838, as a standard gauge building. Eight years later the company was absorbed by the West Cornwall Railway, who converted the shed for broad gauge use. In 1876, the WCR was itself absorbed by the GWR, who re-introduced standard gauge at the end of 1870s! Further improvements were made around the mid-1890s, and Carn Brea continued in use until August 1917, mainly providing 'engines for the goods-only branch to Portreath. Even after closure the shed continued to stand, as this early 1930s picture shows. The two furthermost roads were the loco shed, while the third section of the building, here seen trackless, was a wagon shop. Final demolition probably occurred in the late 1930s.

J. A. Sommerfield Collection

Plates 62 & 63: Cheltenham (High Street), above, circa 1930, with an MSWJ 4-4-0 in residence. This was the second shed on this site, replacing an 1893 single-road depot in 1911. After the Grouping, the GWR eventually decided there was no need for two sheds in Cheltenham. Accordingly, closure came at the end of December 1935, with High Street Shed subsequently being used for non-railway purposes. The photograph below shows it in 1976, in varied use as a grocery warehouse, carpet store and car repair shop. It continues in private service today, in a very good state of preservation.

Author's Collection & Author

Plate 64: Cheltenham (Malvern Road) on the brilliant morning of 8th October 1950. As can be seen the shed is in two sections, with the Churchward 1907 brick building on the right and, on the left, the 1943 corrugated structure, added due to the demands of wartime traffic, especially over the MSWJ route. Outside the shed, from left to right, is Railcar No. 25, Nos. 4141 and 5336 with, in the yard, 'Jinty' No. 47237, from Gloucester (Midland Region) Shed. Inside the shed are: Nos 2254, 2823, 3204, 4534, 4564, 5530 and 6341. Malvern Road Depot closed in September 1963, but part remains today, in industrial use.

T. J. Edgington

Plate 65: Wartime freight. 'Aberdare' No. 2673 blasts past Cheltenham (Malvern Road) Shed on an 'up' goods in March 1945. Sister engine No. 2638, lies beside the depot, failed with a broken crankpin. It was destined never to be repaired, and No. 2638 was withdrawn the following autumn. The various side extensions to the shed were, left to right, offices, stores and, in front of the latter, a sand furnace; surprisingly the depot never was equipped with a turntable.

W. Potter

Plate 66: A 1936 view, from Chester (General) Station platform, looking towards the two buildings of the GWR shed. In front is the 80-year-old original Chester & Birkenhead Railway depot, with GWR gantry coaler and, in the misty distance, the ex-LNWR shed.

B. Matthews

Plate 67: An August 1933 view, of the other (north) end of the C&BR shed, with an unidentified Large Prairie brewing up in no uncertain manner. This building had been re-roofed in 1928, at which time other improvements were made. Being so remote from a workshops facility, the shed's lifting gear was kept busy, to judge by the number of spare wheel sets on hand.

W. R. Dyer Collection

Plate 68: Ex-ROD 2-8-0 No. 3040 receives attention to its driving axle and pony truck at Chester, in July 1935. 'Built like a battleship' would seem to be an apt description, with the side steps being fixed to the running plate by no fewer than sixteen rivets!

W. Potter

Plate 69: A general view of the locomotive yard, looking north between Chester's two sheds, on 17th July 1955. The ex-LNWR depot, with its ornate and varying entrances, was very much in use at that time, after a somewhat chequered history. Vacated by the LNWR in 1870, when that company moved to its new eight-road shed, east of the city, the building served in a number of guises — one of which was a gasworks — until the GWR annexed it for much needed accommodation. The date of annexation is unknown, but in *Plate 66* the depot would appear to have been in use in 1936.

W. Potter

Plate 70: A close-up of Mogul No. 4376 standing beside the ex-LNWR building on 16th June 1935. One shed entrance, at least, is firmly closed, so was all the building in use at that time? The side extension, in lighter-coloured brick, was the office/stores block.

G. Coltas

Plate 71: In 1957, BR re-roofed the old LNWR shed, retaining the separate entrances at the north end. Once again its use for locomotives seems to have ceased, with only wagons being resident thereafter, until closure to steam came in April 1960. By 1st May of that year, when this picture was taken, the re-roofed LNWR building was being adapted for diesel use. This involved new inspection pits and opening-out the arched entrances — temporary supports for the north end's new lintel can clearly be seen through the shed. The ex-C&BR steam shed was also later re-roofed and both buildings survive today, in use for diesels, with this one bearing a 1957 date, although having walls that are, in reality, at least 130 years old!

W. T. Stubbs

Plate 72: Seen from an 'up' train, on 16th June 1957, is the 99-year-old ex-broad gauge depot at Chippenham, a sub-shed of Swindon. A large covered coal stage once stood outside the shed entrance but only a small wagon canopy remains, and even that was soon to be removed. An 0-6-0PT, No. 9600, was being coaled for its next duties, possibly on the Calne branch, which diverged from the 'down' main line immediately opposite the shed. Chippenham Shed closed in March 1964.

L. B. Lapper courtesy N. E. Preedy

Plate 73: The Cheltenham & GW Union Railway opened its delightful broad gauge line from Kemble to Cirencester on 31st May 1841, the shed at the terminus being the first GWR branch line depot. Initially a sub-shed of Swindon, it later became subordinate to Gloucester. However, with typical railway idiosyncrasy, so beloved by us all, the locomotives were always supplied by Swindon! The wooden building in this picture, seen on 2nd June 1936, was an 1872 replacement for the broad gauge shed; it closed in April 1964.

B. Matthews

Plate 74: A 1936 view of the concrete-built shed at Cleobury Town, on the Cleobury Mortimer & Ditton Priors Railway. The CMDPR opened in 1908 and initially the company's locomotives used a shed built by the contractor who constructed the line. This obviously temporary structure lasted nine years before it was replaced by the depot seen here and which was itself closed in July 1938. Thereafter engines were supplied by Kidderminster Shed.

W. A. Camwell

Plate 75: The Barry Railway's goods depot at Bridgend & Coity was provided with a two-road loco shed in 1897. However, most traffic was handled by the depots at Barry and Trehafod, so Coity Junction (as it was called) was not much used. Accordingly, closure came after only nine years, following which the building became a goods shed, serving in that role until well into BR times. The 'northlight'-roofed shed is seen here, circa 1906, with, in residence, 0-6-2T No. 239 (later to become GWR No. 234).

B. Matthews Collection

Plate 76: Brick floors and filled-in pits, remnants of the Taff Vale Railway's railmotor shed at Coke Ovens (Pontypridd). This was built in 1905 and closed in 1927, after which it served as a carriage shed for about seven years. Immediately to the left of the distant signal box had stood the TVR's four-road Coke Ovens loco shed, opened in 1896 and closed on New Years Eve, 1933. Bill Camwell's picture was taken circa 1936, so demolition of both buildings had, for those days, been uncharacteristically swift — only the sheds' water tanks have survived.

W. A. Camwell

Plate 77: A Great Western outpost at the heart of the LNWR's empire. Crewe (Gresty Lane) was a GWR/LNWR joint depot, and the shed was built in the standard LNWR hipped roof style of the period — 1870. It had the unique distinction of being subordinate to two main sheds — Wellington on the GWR and the LNWR's Crewe North. The last-named usually supplied only a couple of engines for Whitchurch and Shrewsbury workings, whereas the GWR's considerable services over its line from Wellington required a larger allocation — seven locomotives in 1901 and six in 1921, for instance. Almost certainly, the traditional inter-railway rivalries, which were continued into BR times, ensured the shed's survival until mid-June 1963. It is seen here on 25th March 1962, with Wrexham's No. 41232 still sporting the old BR emblem. Also on shed that day were Nos 6866/79, 6925/45, 7915, 9741 and 75025.

J. A. Sommerfield

Plate 78: Opening Croes Newydd Shed in 1902 — the last Dean turntable unit to be built — enabled the GWR to close three old and scattered small sheds. These were Brymbo, Summerhill and Trevor (Pontcysyllte), and their duties were concentrated at the new depot. Situated in a triangle of lines south of Wrexham Station, Croes Newydd was necessarily cramped, as may be appreciated from this July 1950 photograph, which shows how close to the shed the coal stage was placed. Nos 5774 and 6694 stand in front of the wartime ash shelter, with the shed's 'northlight' roof just visible on the right. Taken over by the Midland Region in 1963, Croes Newydd had four years of housing Standards and Staniers before closing in March 1967.

B. Hilton

Plate 79: Main depot of the Rhondda & Swansea Bay Railway, Danygraig's west end is seen in 1936. The sections, left to right, are four-road loco shed, repair shop, and carriage and wagon shop. This was a fascinating depot as it housed many of the 'oddities' inherited by the GWR from a number of companies operating in the Swansea area. For example, at nationalisation, the shed had the following types allocated: 0-4-0T (6), 0-4-0ST (6), 0-6-0T (1), 0-6-0ST (3), 0-6-0PT (11), 0-6-2T (2), 0-8-2T (1), 2-8-0T (1); a total of 31 locomotives of eight different types. The shed closed to steam on 4th January 1960 and some years later, the diesel locomotives too moved away, but the buildings survive, in use by the Civil Engineer's Department.

B. Matthews

Plate 80: The interior of the lofty repair shop at Danygraig, on 7th June 1953, with Neath's No. 4576 and Duffryn Yard's No. 1622 among the engines receiving attention. The line-shafting powering the 30 ton gantry crane is clearly visible above and to the left of No. 4576's cab.

B. Hilton

Plates 81 & 82: Two distant glimpses of the three-road wooden shed at Didcot, opened in July 1857, to replace the original broad gauge depot. The picture above dates from 6th October 1930, and shows 'Barnum' class No. 3210, and an outside-framed 0-6-0PT posing by the old coaling plant. Below, in 1931, 'Duke' class No. 3269 *Dartmoor*, and one of her sisters, are seen, on the other side of the coaler, which had been superseded by a new installation out of picture, to the right. However, the twin water tanks of 45,000 gallons total capacity were still in use.

Dr J. Hollick, (Author's Collection) & G. Coltas

Plate 83: The spark-arresting chimney fitted to the pannier tank, seen in *Plate 81*, enabled it to work in the massive military stores depot, set up outside Didcot during World War I. This was a major duty for Didcot's shunters, with up to no fewer than eight pilots employed on the ordnance depot's internal trackage, which totalled an amazing near-eighty miles. These duties were continued by the next shed, a four-road 'Loans Act' depot, opened in August 1932. This picture shows that building two months after opening, with the coal stage and 74,000 gallon tank on the left. A repair shop was sited at the rear of the depot, as was the turntable. This shed's subsequent fate is of course well-known. Closed in June 1965, it now houses the Great Western Society and its many historic artefacts.

BR/OPC

Plate 84: The Brecon & Merthyr Railway had no luck with its Dowlais area loco sheds. The first depot, at Pant, burned down in 1887, so the B&M took over the redundant LNWR shed at Ivor Junction, which served until 1898, when the B&M opened a new shed at Dowlais Central. That corrugated-iron building collapsed in 1916, during a March blizzard! A replacement, in brick, appeared on the same site and it is that building which is depicted, on 26th August 1951, with No. 292, sitting in characteristic Dowlais drizzle. However, note the new brickwork above the coal wagon — had there been yet another mishap? The shed closed in May 1960, but was not immediately demolished, so by September 1962 the shed decided to do it itself, and the roof caved in!

W. Potter

Plate 85: A 1936 view of Duffryn Yard Shed, with the original 'northlight' roof still intact. Built by the Port Talbot Railway in 1896, the GWR made improvements to locomotive accommodation in 1931 that included the opening up of the previously-unused sixth shed road. These changes allowed closure of a life-expired shed at Aberavon. Having the distinction of an all-tank engine allocation for most — if not all — of its life, Duffryn Yard closed in March 1964.

B. Matthews

Plate 86: To coin the old adage, 'If you can't see the mountains it is raining, but if you can see the mountains, it is about to rain'! The rear of Duffryn Yard on 4th May 1952, with congestion causing locomotives to be parked on the access road to the 55ft. turntable. Not that that mattered, as it was a Sunday, so nothing was going to move anyway! In the distance, immediately right of No. 6717, is the 1931 repair shop and, right of that, the 20,000 gallon water tank with shed offices behind.

L. B. Lapper courtesy N. E. Preedy

Plate 87: An 'up' goods train is about to cross the River Avon and pass Evesham Shed. It is the late 1950s and almost certainly a Sunday, as Nos 6338 and 9429, both from the parent shed of Worcester, appear lifeless, as do their anonymous sisters. The brick-built shed, with tiled roof, opened in 1901 as a replacement for an ex-Oxford, Wolverhampton & Worcester Railway depot at the station, which incidentally, consisted of an arch of a road overbridge, with a dead-end extension building. Just out of picture, to the left, the former MR line from Ashchurch bridged the Avon and entered that company's own station which also had a loco shed for many years. Evesham GWR depot closed in June 1961.

W. Potter

Plate 88: With the failure of Brunel's atmospheric system, the South Devon Railway used borrowed locomotives for a while and, at Exeter, housed them in a hurriedly built shed at the west end of the 'down' side of the station. Not much else is known, except that, in the early 1860s, the SDR depot was probably converted for use as a carriage shed. From an undated anonymous copy negative we see a strangely deserted station forecourt at Exeter, with, in the left distance, a building that looks suspiciously like a three-road engine shed. The author offers nothing more than conjecture — on a date, circa 1875, and that the building in the background *is* the ex-SDR locomotive depot — by that time a carriage shed.

Author's Collection

Plates 89 & 90: Rebuilding of Exeter Station, 1862-4, was accompanied by erection of the B&ER's third loco shed. The first, a temporary structure, serving from 1844 to 1851, was superseded by a three-road depot which stood on the north side of the station. The third building, seen above in the early 1930s, was built opposite the 1851 shed and faced west. The shed is as extended in the mid-1890s by the GWR, with the period 'northlight' roof still in remarkably good condition. However, further ravages, of time and World War II, caused the roof to be replaced, as was seen below, on 1st September 1955. Notice the coal stage is not topped by the customary tank — that was positioned out of picture to the left, on its own tankhouse, roughly on the site of the B&ER's 1851 shed. Some of the locomotives visible were, by the coaler, Nos 90563, 5021 *Whittington Castle* and 6360, and stabled in the shed entrances, Nos 1449, 9439 and 75028. The shed site remains in use today, as a diesel stabling point, complete with most of the depot's walls, now some 124 years old.

A. G. Ellis & W. Potter

Plate 91: A close-up of the re-roofed shed at Exeter, on 20th April 1962, eighteen months before closure to steam. Nos 3794, 3709 and 1449 have some ropey-looking coal on board and the staypost on the water crane beside the 0-4-2T seems to be under a certain amount of strain! No. 3709's chimney is noteworthy — was it a temporary replacement, following an accident, or was it an experiment in draughting, possibly in an effort to coerce that dreadful coal into combustion?

T. W. Nicholls

Plate 92: Next day, 21st April 1962, Exeter's weather had changed and, above the buffer stop, the River Exe looks menacingly swollen. A railway enthusiast, predictably attired in raincoat, scarf, 'ballast-crusher' boots and camera, points out something important to No 7316's fireman, who listens with a slightly amused expression on his face! Notice the driver's classic pose, with hand on reversing lever, clutching the obligatory rag. At least the coal seems to be of better quality! Exeter's 65ft. manual turntable is a typically Great Western over-girder type, with hand-wheel locking and neat step ladder down into the shallow pit. Between the sand furnace and high-roofed repair shop No. 5098 *Clifford Castle* patiently simmers, awaiting her next duty.

T. W. Nicholls

Plate 93: A Fairford engineman poses proudly by his two commendably clean charges, Nos 7411 and 4513, on 6th August 1950. The neat little wooden shed was built by the East Gloucestershire Railway in 1873, when that company extended the Oxford to Witney branch to Fairford. The EGR was absorbed by the GWR in 1890, and the shed survived for a further 72 years until closure in June 1962. A factory now covers its site.

T. J. Edgington

Plate 94: The rarely-photographed two-road stone-built shed at Falmouth was an unusually early casualty, being closed on 21st September 1925, after 62 years service. The building was finally demolished sometime around 1933, but its site remained a locomotive stabling point until the end of steam. The stabling point is seen in the early 1960s with one paved shed road, a pit, 7,000 gallon tank, water crane and a couple of ancillary buildings having survived for some 30 years.

W. T. Stubbs Collection

Plate 95: Originally broad gauge, Faringdon Shed opened with the Faringdon Railway's line from Uffington, in 1864, to be taken over by the GWR 22 years later. The shed closed in December 1951, but being of robust construction it survived, in private use. Seen here from across the abandoned station platform, on 27th September 1964, it is employed as a garage by the Express Dairy. The small side extension, rapidly becoming overgrown, was the office.

W. T. Stubbs Collection

Plate 96: Needing to cope with increasing traffic, the Taff Vale Railway replaced the original single road shed at Ferndale with a four-road depot, in 1884. About 1932 the GWR demolished one of the shed's two-road bays, retaining one open track and building an office block over the other. At the same time a corrugated-clad coaling gantry was installed and that is seen below, on 17th June 1951, partly obscuring the shed's wooden gable-end. The right-hand pit, spur with locomotive No. 293, office block and new brickwork at the top of the right-hand wall, clearly mark the position of the erstwhile second bay. Final closure occurred in September 1964.

L. B. Lapper courtesy N. E. Preedy

Plate 97: Goodwick village, in 1936, forms a backdrop to the loco shed that was opened, together with nearby Fishguard Harbour, as a result of the GWR's quest for a share of the lucrative Irish boat traffic. The second Churchward straight shed to be built, this two-road depot was laid out in 1906, in such a way as to permit easy expansion, should traffic warrant. Witness the open tracks to the left of the shed, over which a further two-road section could be erected. There was an easily replaceable corrugated coaling stage and 12,000 gallon tank, which had an unusual pitched-roof wagon shelter. An over-girder turntable, just visible on the shed's right, completed the facilities. Alas, the hoped-for traffic levels never were attained and the shed closed, as built, in September 1963.

B. Matthews

Plate 98: Frome sported an engine shed for 109 years, between 1854 and 1963. Originally the depot was longer than the 60ft. building seen here on 11th October 1953, so some reduction or replacement (the latter, probably) had been made, at a date not yet determined. With its closure pre-dating Beeching, Frome Shed remained busy to the end, with as many as a dozen locomotives allocated, for shunting and local trips, branch services to Radstock, Shepton Mallet and Wells, and over the main line to Westbury and Yeovil. As can be seen, two open-air pits were provided, the nearest probably having once been inside the original building, while coaling was carried out from wagons on the furthest. The goods sidings passing behind the depot were often used for weekend stabling.

B. Hilton

Plate 99: Pride in the job! Gloucester, about 1900, with the 1854 four-road shed in the background. The building had opened in replacement of the May 1845 depot, built when the Cheltenham & GW Union Railway first arrived in the city. From 1848, until closure, only goods engines were housed at the first shed, with the passenger engine stud at Cheltenham.

B. Hilton Collection

Plate 100: Gloucester (Horton Road), as it was additionally known, in BR days, on 8th June 1955, showing the four-road shed little changed from some 55 years previously. On its left is the 1872 six-road extension and left, of that again, the stone-built repair shop, which was equipped with a wheel-drop. This marks the approximate position of the small diesel depot erected after Gloucester steam shed closed in December 1965.

W. Potter

Plate 101: Gloucester's coal stage, topped by a 74,000 gallon tank, seen on 16th July 1949, with Class 1901 0-6-0PT No. 2009 on pilot duties. Just visible behind the pannier tank is the corrugated-iron extension to the stage, added in 1943, to allow 'both sides' coaling.

W. Potter

Plates 102 & 103: The GWR had been working the Vale of Neath Railway since 1865, and by 1879, found it necessary to provide a banking engine shed at Glyn Neath. The southern end of those basic facilities is seen above, in August 1936. One thing that is immediately apparent is the close similarity of the shed to that at Bath (*see Plate 28*), i.e. an elevated tank, with walled-in space beneath. Because covered accommodation was so scant, the shed was extended in the following year, by addition of an 80ft. brick shed; the covered coaling platform was enlarged at the same time. The extended shed is seen below on 18th April 1960, with No. 4275 outside, waiting the next banking duty. Inside, were Nos 3741, 8775, 4242 and 4281. Decreasing traffic and increasing dieselisation gradually rendered the bankers redundant, so the shed closed on 5th October 1964. Today, the entire railway 'over the hill' is just a memory.

W. A. Camwell & J. Peden

Plate 104: There is some uncertainty about the opening and closing dates of the small shed at Hayle. It might have been built as early as 1843, by the Hayle Railway, or in 1879, by the GWR. Similarly, closure seems to have been in the mid-1890s, about the time the (other?) Hayle Railway shed at Carn Brea was improved, but 'officially' Hayle was not taken out of use until 1906. This picture shows the neat little stone building trackless, and slowly wasting away, sometime in the early 1930s. Demolition date is unknown, but probably was at the end of that decade. The track in the foreground was the steeply graded branch to Hayle Harbour.

J. A. Sommerfield Collection

Plate 105: The Helston Railway opened its branch from Gwinear Road on 9th May 1887; the GWR worked the line from the outset and fully absorbed it in 1898. Typically, branch services commenced each day from Helston, so a locomotive was housed overnight at the terminus, in the small granite shed seen here on 27th August 1957, with No. 4540 in residence. Steam haulage finished in September 1962, but although the shed's usefulness ended at that time, it was not officially closed until December 1963.

A. R. Goult

Plate106: It has been published before, but Mr Casserley's picture of Hemyock engine shed deserves to be seen again. It was all there, on that beautiful afternoon in May 1929. With the day's work done and about to go on shed, is the elderly but lovingly cared-for branch engine, an ex-South Devon Railway 2-4-0T, No. 1300. The driver is also about to go home, with bicycle clips fixed, dirty overall under his arm, and tea bottle and lunch tin to be stowed on his bike. Behind the engine are the ashes of today's and previous services, with fire iron casually resting against the carriage shed wall, below which can be seen the wheels of the ancient coach that No. 1300 has just ambled up with, from Tiverton Junction. A moment in time, and we are indeed fortunate that Mr Casserley was there to capture it in his classic photograph. For, only five months later, Hemyock Shed was closed, and No. 1300 moved away, to subsequently meet its fate. However the water tank survived, to be repositioned by the station platform.

H. C. Casserley

Plate 107: Destined to serve only 14 years, from its opening in June 1894, was the small shed at Henley-in-Arden. Its short operating life was due to the building of a new line from Bearley, through Henley, to Tyseley, which effectively isolated the original terminus. This subsequently became a goods depot, and it is seen in that role, with the abandoned shed still standing, circa 1936.

W. A. Camwell

Plate 108: Henley-on-Thames was reached by the GWR's branch from Twyford in 1857. A small shed was provided, adjoining the station, much in the same way as at Uxbridge (Vine Street). Henley-on-Thames soon became an outer part of the stockbroker belt, so, in later years, the shed — or at least its turntable — was used for such illustrious types as 'Castles' and 'Halls'. These were provided for the prestigious weekday return commuter train, that often loaded to ten coaches or more, and ran non-stop between Henley and Paddington. The more mundane services were, of course, handled by tank engines, of which one was normally sub-shedded from Reading. The shed is pictured here, slowly decaying, on 19th September 1963, five years after closure. Houses now cover its site and vandals — within and without BR — have ensured the station did not retain its marvellous roof!

W. T. Stubbs Collection

Plates 109 to 111: Hereford (Barton) Shed, former main depot of the Newport, Abergavenny & Hereford Railway, was built in 1853, and taken over by the GWR in 1869. The GWR immediately closed its own 14-year-old two-road shed, opposite Barrs Court Station (but which subsequently saw another 70-80 years service as a carriage shed), and concentrated all locomotive activities at Barton. The solidly-built NAHR depot was little changed and it is seen above, from the rear, about 1946, with a number of different locomotive types on view, including a shiny 'Saint' and an 'Austerity' 2-8-0, No. 2744. The shed's original roof was in need of repair, and this had been effected by the time the very wet front view of the shed was taken, on 23rd August 1953 (centre). The LMS locomotive types visible were a legacy of the days when both the MR and LNWR had sheds at Hereford. Those were closed in 1924 and 1938 respectively, after which their engines gravitated to the GWR depot. Another LNWR/LMS type is seen in the lower picture, standing in the coal line, on 13th April 1957. An 0-8-0, No. 49422 had recently been transferred from Tredegar (86K) to Pontypool Road (86G), but obviously the latter shed did not have a spare shed plate, so a stencilled 'G', and white-painted '86' from its old plate had to suffice!

Woodfin Collection, Courtesy of Bristol City Museum, W. T. Stubbs Collection & W. Potter

Plate 112: In 1907, the GWR had to remove Honeybourne's 1859 OW&WR shed, for track widening. Four years later the replacement shed burned down so the GWR gave up! Subsequent locomotive facilities, for over 54 years, consisted solely of a coaling platform and locomans cabin. No. 2289 stands by the coal stage on 26th June 1960.

K. Fairey

Plate 113: Opened by the Oswestry & Newtown Railway, in March 1863, the shed at the terminus of the Abermule to Kerry branch survived take-over by the Great Western Railway, to close in 1931. It then existed for many more years, as evidenced by this scene of 19th August 1955. Housing one small tank engine before closure, engines for the regular goods train, invariably 0-6-0s of Cambrian or GWR 'Dean Goods' varieties, were subsequently supplied by Moat Lane.

T. J. Edgington

Plates 114 & 115: Seen above in the snowy February of 1932, the year of its closure, is the 80-year-old ex-OW&WR depot at Kidderminster Life-expired, and with an allocation of some twenty engines far exceeding the shed's capabilities, replacement was long overdue. The restrictions of the site are made more apparent in the lower picture, which shows the coaling shelter in 1931 with ex-Llanelly & Mynydd Mawr Railway 0-6-0T, No. 803, substituting for one of the CMDPR engines, away at Works. The shelter was on the shed road, while the 2-6-2T partly visible on the left stood on a stabling road, with the 'up' loop to the left of that. Behind the camera, a 42ft. turntable had, until 1899, cut into the embankment. Today, this shed's location may just be made out by passengers travelling on the Severn Valley Railway, on the right, as they enter that railway's new Kidderminster station.

BR/OPC & G. Coltas

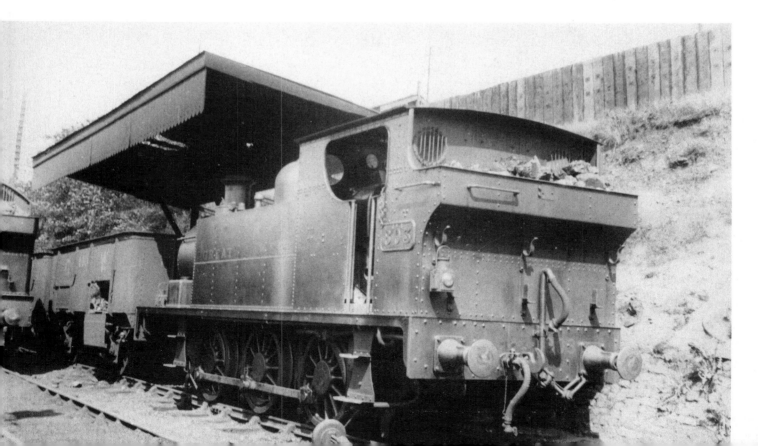

Plates 116 & 117: The 1932 replacement shed at Kidderminster, in February of that year, sited in much more spacious surroundings, south of the line to Bridgnorth. Readers will recall that this building formerly stood at Bassaleg (B&M) — *see Plate 27*, being re-erected under the 'Loans Act', and in its new role at Kidderminster has a slightly modified smoke vent and brick-built offices down one wall. Below, in 1948, ex-CM&DPR No. 29 is seen in the shed yard, with a dwindling coal stack behind. The temporary looking wooden coal stage, with 22,000 gallon tank, seems to have stood the test of time fairly well. Closed in August 1964 and subsequently demolished, the shed's site may also be made out by passengers travelling on the SVR.

BR/OPC & W. Potter

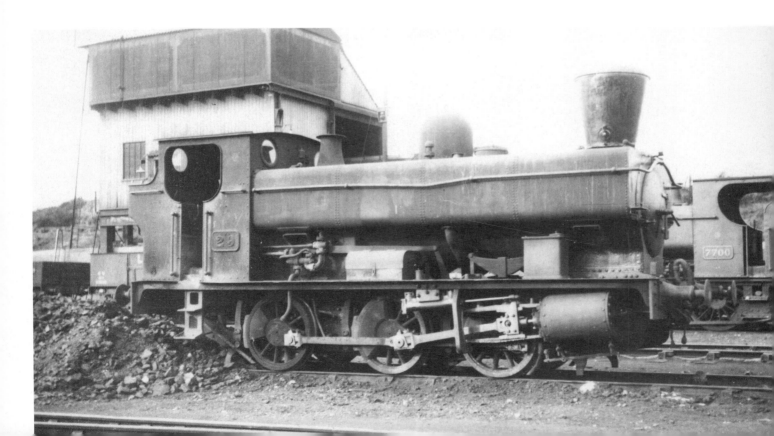

Plate 118: Author's licence! Kidwelly Tinplate Works' loco shed was not one-time Gwendraeth Valley Railway property, but the shed's resident most certainly was. Seeing the light of day for the first time in months, on 7th July 1947, was ex-GVR 0-6-0ST No. 2 (ex-GWR No. 1378). She continued to languish in the shed for some years, until happily preserved by a local council. The GVR's Kidwelly Shed, opened in 1905 and closed in 1923, stood only a few hundred yards away from the tinplate works.

H. C. Casserley

Plate 119: Kingham Station was originally called Chipping Norton Junction, and had a small wooden engine shed from 1881 to 1906. A replacement building was erected in 1913, to stand for nearly fifty years, before it too was closed. That neat little shed is depicted on 11th May 1957 with, as usual, the resident locomotive (No. 78001) outside, and a wagon inside! The embankment in the background carried the late-lamented Cheltenham to Banbury line.

W. Potter

Plate 120: All GWR enthusiasts regretted the demise, in September 1961, of the Brent to Kingsbridge line — the quintessential GWR West Country branch line. Opened in 1893, the terminus occupied a curving restricted site, so the shed, solidly built in granite, had to occupy a small corner, tucked away behind the goods dock. Shed, 12,000 gallon tank and coal platform are seen about 1937, with Class 4575 2-6-2T No. 4585 and one of her sisters in attendance.

W. A. Camwell

Plate 121: No. 4985 *Allesley Hall* uses the 55ft. over-girder turntable at Kingswear on 26th May 1958. There had been a Dartmouth & Torbay Railway (South Devon Railway) shed here from 1864 to 1924, and this turntable and sidings were put down to supplement it. That was in 1900 and entailed the use of land that had, in part, been reclaimed from the Dart estuary.

K. Fairey

Plate 122: Author's licence again! Kinnerley Junction loco shed was never part of the GWR's empire but, being in GWR 'territory' with, on this occasion, a 100 per cent ex-GWR allocation, it qualifies! It was built by the eccentric Shropshire & Montgomeryshire Railway, which rose from the ashes of the even more eccentric Potteries, Shrewsbury & North Wales Railway. But the War Department was the first to put the line to major use, during wartime, serving a number of military depots. This picture was taken in May 1947 and still in WD service are, from left to right, ex-GWR 'Dean Goods' Nos 70169, 70197, 70180 and 70196 — (formerly GWR Nos 2479, 2540, 2514 and 2576 respectively). The War Department closed the shed in 1960.

W. Potter

Plate 123: Plymouth (Laira) Shed on 29th May 1958, looking south from the hillside. The double track curving from left, to the bottom right, is the GWR line between Lipson and Mount Gould Junctions; the LSWR had running powers over this route to reach that company's terminus at Friary. A single track from mid-right, to bottom right, is the GWR connection from Laira Junction, providing a useful triangle for turning locomotives. At Laira Depot, in front of the straight shed, on the left, the boiler washout plant is visible, while right of that are the oil tanks. These had been put up for the short-lived oil-firing venture, were used again during the Western Region's flirtation with gas turbines (the 'Kerosene Castles'!), and once more, in the first days of dieselisation, before a diesel depot was built on the land occupied by a pond and coal yard, on the extreme right of the picture. Finally the coal stage and its extensions are readily apparent.

K. Fairey

Plate 124: Laira's first shed, the penultimate Dean turntable unit, was opened in 1901 to relieve the congested 1849 ex-South Devon Railway depot at Millbay, which did not finally close until 1931. The sand shed stands immediately left of the distant depot entrance, while the offices are located behind the hoist. In this scene of 27th June 1960, after 59 years service, the shed's 'northlight' roof has, not surprisingly, lost its original tiles in favour of corrugated materials.

W. Potter

SALUTE TO A CAMERAMAN

An old friend of the author's, prize-winning photographer Terry Nicholls, spent the first years of his railway career at Laira, before moving to Bristol. Terry would not argue, I think, when I say his time at Laira has, so far, been the highlight of his working life. So, as a lasting tribute, Terry set out with his camera, in the early 1960s, to record as much as he could of the shed's atmosphere, before it disappeared forever. It is my pleasure to present six of Terry's works now, as my dual tribute — to the railwayman photographer, and his depot.

Plate 125: Two in one! While not perfectly joined, Terry's pictures superbly capture the spectacle of a turntable shed's interior. Half of Laira's 24 stabling roads are seen, on 15th April 1962, with, among the tank engines, Nos 1003 *County of Wilts,* 6988 *Swithland Hall,* 6938 *Corndean Hall,* 5000 *Launceston Castle* and 4087 *Cardigan Castle.*

Plate 126: Finally allowing closure of Millbay Depot, a 'Loans Act' shed was erected at Laira in 1931, and christened the 'Long' shed. Seen on 22nd April 1962, to the right of the four-road shed is the stores building, while on the left of the oil tanks is an auto-coach, then being used as an office. Locomotives on view are, left to right, Nos 4927 *Farnborough Hall,* 6955 *Lydcott Hall,* 6834 *Dummer Grange,* 1008 *County of Cardigan,* 1028 *County of Warwick,* 5082 *Swordfish* and 3862. For the record, other locomotives on shed that day were, Nos 1003/4, 1363, 3852, 4082/7/95, 4555/61/6/7, 4658, 4705/6, 4972/82, 5024/9/65, 5512/32/41/4/64/8/9/72, 5913, 6015, 6771, 6809/15/60/3/73, 7006/14/22, 7916 and 9467 — total 50.

Plate 127: An inspiring vista from inside the 'Long' shed on 11th March 1962 — four classes in one photograph! From left to right, also in ascending order of tractive effort, are Nos 7909 *Heveningham Hall,* 6826 *Nannerth Grange,* 5014 *Goodrich Castle* and 6019 *King Henry V.* In those days, scenes like this could make one believe that steam would last forever, but already the harbinger of doom is visible. The diesel depot in the background which, with its locomotive inhabitants, was to write finis to Laira steam shed, in April 1964, and eventually to all this magnificent quartet.

Plate 128: Double trouble! Class 4500 locomotives Nos. 4567 and 4574 receive attention under the hoist, on 11th March 1962. Laira usually had eight to ten of these useful engines, of both marques, whose speed and power made them ideal for local and branch line services, especially over the long and hilly route to Tavistock and Launceston.

Plate 129: Laira's original coal stage and 45,000 gallon tank, on 11th February 1962. No. 5532 is officiating (specially posed, more like!), while a sunbathed No. 1006 *County of Cornwall* looks on. Behind the 'County' is the wartime extension to the coaler, which obscures an earlier enlargement, made in 1931, in brick, for the opening of the 'Long' shed.

Plate 130: Atmosphere at Landore in 1936, with the 'Old' shed in the background. This had been built in 1874, superseding an 1850 South Wales Railway shed at Swansea (High Street). However, the SWR building outlived its successor by seeing more than a century of further use as part of a goods shed.

Author's Collection

Plate 131: From an unfortunately deteriorated negative, Landore's 'New' shed is seen not long after completion, in 1932. A four-road 'Loan Act' building, it had all the usual facilities, like the repair shop on the left, with the boiler house in front, and much improved working conditions for the men. 'Old' and 'New' sheds were replaced in the early 1960s by a diesel depot.

BR/OPC

Plate 132: It's a 'Shedbash Sunday' in South Wales and, as usual, it's raining! Both Landore sheds are visible on 4th May 1952, with a raincoated legion of the faithful plodding about, all 'doing' the shed in their own way. Holding centre-stage is No. 5016 *Montgomery Castle*, temporarily laid up, it seems. A few years later she was one of Landore's star performers, kept in pristine order for the best turns. The author has vivid memories of this locomotive's bustling performance on an 'up' 'South Wales Pullman' in 1957, when a certain 100m.p.h. (the driver claimed 105) was attained at Little Somerford. Halcyon days!

W. Potter

Plate 133: It is 12th September 1970, and Landore has been a diesel depot for years, but the breakdown crane is still steam and it has a history, as the ex-SR crew coach might hint. A Cowans Sheldon product, of 36 tons capacity, the crane was originally delivered to the LSWR in 1922, as that company's No. 7. Allocated to Salisbury, it was renumbered 37S by the Southern Railway, and stayed in Wiltshire's County Town for 45 years. Leaving, on the closure of Salisbury Shed in July 1967, the crane moved to the Western Region, at Worcester, where it was de-rated to 32 tons and renumbered 376. Eventually moved to Landore, Crane No. 376 was finally withdrawn and scrapped during 1970/1.

P. Tatlow

Plate 134: Launceston's attractive shed, built in random-stone in 1865, and depicted here in June 1954. All facilities except the turntable are seen, and were little changed in the shed's 97 years of service, except for a small lengthening of the building in 1899. The lines on the left of the picture led to the GWR station, while on the right, beyond the buffer stop, is the LSWR's North Cornwall main line.

E. V. Fry

Plate 135: Leamington's four-road depot was the prototype of Churchward's straight shed design, opening in 1906, to replace an 1852 shed which burned down in 1902. In this view, from 6th October 1936, Leamington is seen with some of the passenger tanks that usually made up most of its allocation of about 25 locomotives. Closure came in June 1965, after a couple of years as a Midland Region depot.

B. Matthews

Plate 136: Banking engines were provided at Ledbury because 'up' trains faced a climb of four miles to a summit east of Colwall. To service the bankers, basic coal, water and fire-cleaning facilities were installed in the early 1860s, with a turntable being added later. There appears never to have been a shed building, but this small stabling point was officially classed as a sub-shed of Hereford. It is seen here on 11th July 1959, with 2-8-0T No. 5243 as resident banker. Dieselisation resulted in closure during mid-1964.

W. Potter

Plate 137: Leominster Shed was opened in 1853 by the Shrewsbury & Hereford Railway, which later became a GWR/LNWR Joint undertaking. However, the depot was used only by the GWR, which replaced the building in 1901. That replacement, the last Dean 'northlight' straight shed, is seen here on 28th April 1935, with residents that would have been typical throughout its 61 years of service — i.e., 0-4-2T and 0-6-0T locomotives. Part of the turntable is visible between the depot and the sand furnace, and behind the latter is the coal platform, which had the luxury of a bucket crane but no covering!

B. Matthews

Plate 138: The penultimate Churchward-style turntable shed to be opened, in March 1925, Llanelly was the last to have multiple turntables — in this case, two. It replaced a Llanelly Dock & Railway Company shed and was provided with a large-size coal stage, 180,000 gallon tank, and a layout that anticipated addition of two further turntables. Such expansion never materialised, and the shed closed, unaltered, on 1st November 1965, three years after this picture was taken.

W. T. Stubbs Collection

Plate 139: The inside of Llanelly Shed, on 17th April 1949, with a quartet of ex-BPGV locomotives in view. Although this appears to be a well-lit interior, the glare of sunlight reflected off the front of the right-hand engine shows just how dark it really was. All the more credit to the photographer for judging his exposure value correctly.

W. Potter

Plate 140: Remotely situated in the hills of north Montgomeryshire, Llangynog was the terminus of the Tanat Valley Light Railway, a Cambrian Railways' subsidiary. There was a loco shed for a few years after opening, in 1904, the remains of which are seen on the right, in this undated photograph. The water tank had a coal platform between its supports and the ash pit probably was situated outside the shed entrance. Little else is known.

OPC

Plate 141: 'Dean Goods' No. 2542 sits inside the shed at Llanidloes in May 1939. This 1864 shed, with its neat little two-storey office building, was sole survivor of three depots that once existed in this small Montgomeryshire town. Between the shed and signal box, a turntable can be seen and, beyond that, a small hut. The latter stands on the site of a single road Mid-Wales Railway depot, also opened in 1864, closed some 40 years later, but not demolished until the early 1930s. Left of the signal box a large tree can be seen, just behind which was the site of Llanidloes' first shed — that of the Llanidloes & Newtown Railway, opened in 1859 and closed in 1864. Llanidloes lost its last shed in December 1962 and, eventually, all of its railways.

B. Matthews Collection

Plate 142: A Dean 'northlight' shed at Llantrisant, in the late 1940s. Opened in October 1900, it replaced an 1860 two-road Ely Valley Railway shed. Locomotives stationed at Llantrisant operated the GWR branches radiating from there and, after the Grouping, took over services on the ex-TVR, ex-Cowbridge Railway route to Aberthaw. Llantrisant Shed closed in its 64th birthday month but diesels continued to stable thereabouts until final closure as a 'train crew depot', in March 1987.

B. Matthews Collection

Plate 143: Looking more like a goods shed, Ludlow engine shed is seen on 5th July 1959, nearly eight years after closure. Of 1857 Shrewsbury & Hereford Railway origins, Ludlow was noteworthy for providing the usually unique types of locomotives for its Clee Hill sub-shed, situated at the top of a one-mile rope incline. The building was converted during 1976/7, becoming part of a warehouse complex.

W. T. Stubbs

Plates 144 & 145: Formerly the headquarters of the Severn & Wye Railway, Lydney Shed was opened in 1868 and saw little alteration in its near 96 years of service. In two views photographed on 7th August 1957, we see above the three-road loco shed, pits and coaling platform. The Class 1600 0-6-0PT was typical of the lightweight locomotives that were a must for some of the S&WR's lines. In the lower picture the delightfully decrepit rear of the shed is seen, with coal stack, repair shop and stationary boiler. The unorthodox water tanks held a total of about 4,500 gallons.

W. Potter

Plates 146 to 148: The ex-Cambrian Railways' shed at Machynlleth, had an unusual 3-road/2-road configuration. In the top picture, photographed on 27th August 1959, we see, looking from the west, stored 'Dukedog' No. 9012 beside the gantry coaler. The 65ft. turntable was sited behind the camera. The centre picture shows the western, three-road end of the shed, in the early 1950s. No. 3202 stands beside the shed offices, above which towers a hillside that obviously had to be hacked away when the shed was built in 1863. The depot's brick gable end indicates that some re-roofing had been done, as the rest of the shed was stone-built. This may be appreciated from the two-road eastern end of the shed, as seen below, on 28th July 1961. No. 7417 stands beside the water tank, with BR Standard Class 2 No. 78007 in the shed entrance. Standard Class 4 4-6-0s were the last type to leave when the shed closed to steam in December 1966. The building survives today, partly roofless, in use by diesels, including the new 'Sprinter' units, making it one of the oldest ex-GWR depots still in use.

W. Potter, B. Matthews Collection & K. Fairey

Plates 149 & 150: The GWR built the Malmesbury Railway in 1877, ran it from the outset, and absorbed it in 1890. Branching from the Wooton Bassett to Chippenham line at Dauntsey, a further connection was later made at Little Somerford, where the Badminton line passed over the Malmesbury Railway. Motive power was invariably an 0-4-2T, and such an engine, No. 5805, is seen above on shed at Malmesbury, on 2nd June 1935. The depot closed in September 1951 but survived demolition, and in the lower view its somewhat 'tatty' remains are seen in 1976, in use as a farmer's store. The remainder of Malmesbury Station's site was, by that time, a small industrial estate.

B. Matthews & Author

Plate 151: Marlborough (High Level) loco shed is seen across the low level ex-SMAR, ex-MSWJ line, on 28th April 1935. Opened by the Marlborough Railway in April 1864, the shed was extended as shown in 1899, and housed engines working the Savernake to Marlborough shuttle. The branch became redundant when the GWR took over the MSWJ line at the Grouping, but with the usual urgency of the time, official closure of the shed was not effected until July 1933.

B. Matthews

Plate 152: Branching from the Wycombe Railway at Bourne End, the Great Marlow Railway's line to the Thames-side town of (Great) Marlow opened in 1872. The one-road shed at the terminus, seen here on 26th September 1954, housed engines working the famous 'Marlow Donkey,' until dieselisation caused closure in July 1962. Obviously the shed's foundations were built to lightweight standards, as a notice outside the door sternly prohibits entry to Red and Blue classified locomotives.

T. J. Edgington

Plates 153 & 154: Like most South Wales valleys towns, Merthyr had, over the years, a complex railway history, including four engine sheds. First to arrive was the Taff Vale Railway, which had two sheds at its station, 1841-1846 and 1846-1923. The Vale of Neath Railway was next, opening its broad gauge line and station in 1854, with workings being taken over by the GWR eleven years later. The GWR replaced the two road VoNR shed in 1877, with a three-road 'northlight' building, on the same site. That shed is seen above, on 25th August 1935; on the right-hand side is the sand house, with offices in the background, and part of the coaling stage canopy. By 1960 (below), the depot had been re-roofed in pitched style, with gable ends, using steel and asbestos. Some extra cladding had also been applied to the gantry coaler, which had No. 5699 sitting outside on that day. Notice too the signalling changes effected in the quarter of a century between the two photographs. Merthyr's last shed closed in November 1964, but remains in private use today.

B. Matthews & C. L. Caddy

Plate 155: Seen above, in April 1954, is the second of two Milford Railway sheds at Milford (Haven), dating from December 1890; the first broad gauge building had been opened in 1863. The Milford Railway was absorbed by the GWR in 1896, with the shed becoming subordinate to Neyland. Milford Haven depot closed, with the end of steam, in December 1962.

E. V. Fry

Plate 156: Minehead's 1874 shed was a further example of a building that served in two locations. For twelve years prior to 1874 it stood at Watchet, terminus of the West Somerset Railway. Moved to Minehead by the Minehead Railway, a leased company of the B&ER, the fabric of the shed was, therefore, 73 years old when this photograph was taken, on 10th June 1935. Closure was in November 1956, but locomotives continued to stable in the shed for some years after. Note the unusual roof feature of a weather vane.

B. Matthews

Plates 157 & 158: All change at Moat Lane Junction! Brian Hilton's two visits, almost exactly seven years apart, record old and new sheds from very similar vantage points. In the top view, dating from 23rd June 1951, the wooden Llanidloes & Newtown Railway's shed is seen, in its 92nd year, and certainly showing its age! By 15th June 1958 (centre), the L&NR's depot had succumbed, to be replaced by this corrugated building, completed in 1957. Dimensions were the same — only the single-pitched roof differed from the original. The 'bashers' have noted the numbers of 46509, 46514 and 46522 and are returning to their coach, for the dash to the next shed — remember those Sundays? Moat Lane's second shed closed in December 1962, after a life of only five years; it survives today, in private use.

B. Hilton

Plate 159: Liskeard & Looe Railway's depot at Moorswater, about 1935. Seemingly, the shed is closed, but that was not the case until September 1962, after 94 years service, latterly as a sub-shed of St. Blazey. The track curving away behind the depot was the former Liskeard & Caradon Railway's line to Cheesewring, high up on the moors. Some enthusiasts consider that the wooden building seen on the left was the L&CR's loco shed, but the author has yet to find evidence that confirms, or refutes this.

B. Matthews

Plates 160 & 161: Built in 1866, the Moretonhampstead & South Devon Railway's line and shed were absorbed by the SDR in 1872, only to be absorbed again, by the GWR, in 1876. There then followed 71 years of service as a remote sub-shed of Newton Abbot, before closure in November 1947. The top view, dating from about 1935, shows the neat little stone building with doors tightly closed against the elements. The small adjoining building was Moretonhampstead signal box. The water tank and coaling platform are seen, but the latter appears not to be in use, with coal dumped on the ground by the shed. Such a sturdy building was bound to survive, and so it did, as can be seen in the lower view, which dates from December 1975. Once again, that politically favoured blight on the face of Britain, the heavy goods lorry, has prevailed!

B. Matthews & Author

Plate 162: The double turntable shed at Neath (Court Sart) was one of the earliest of the GWR's multiple turntable depots, being preceded only by Wolverhampton (Stafford Road). Opened in 1876, Court Sart succeeded a two-road Vale of Neath Railway building nearby, which itself dated from 1862. Relatively little change was effected during Court Sart's years of service, except for provision of a new coaling stage in 1921 and recladding of the roof by BR. The depot is seen here on 2nd June 1926; notice that the five-year-old coal stage is, unusually, stone-built — the tank held 90,000 gallons.

BR/OPC

Plate 163: This view shows one of Neath's breakdown train's vans, in close-up. The date is early BR, and the match truck next to No. W119 has just been labelled 'W120'. Both vehicles accompanied 20 ton steam crane No. 4 (Cowans Sheldon 1903), which was stationed at Neath at the time. Only after such things are gone do most of us realise what we ignored, as we bustled round the sheds, grabbing locomotive numbers and photographs. What price one of these vans nowadays? What price that superb all-wood carriage board even!

Woodfin Collection, Courtesy of Bristol City Museum

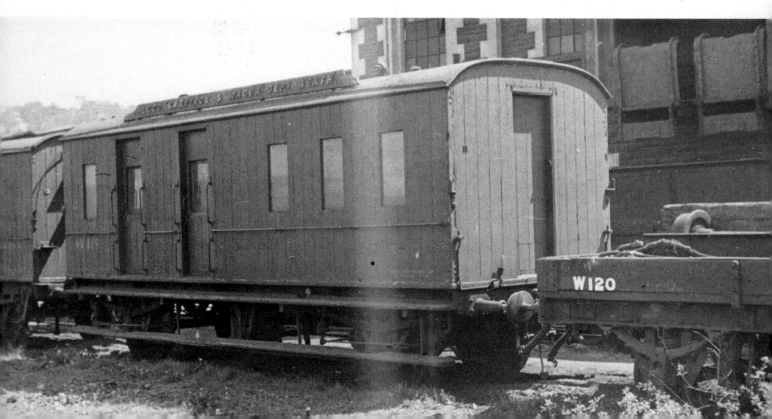

Plates 164 & 165: Two interior shots of Neath (Court Sart), taken on 16th May 1965, a month before closure. The view above, looking across the shed at Pannier tanks around both turntables, is wonderfully cluttered! A wooden cabin visible behind No. 3647 was more or less standard, but this is the first time the author has seen a grounded wagon body and PW-type huts *inside* a loco shed! The roof construction is noteworthy and the 'rivet counters' will have a field day with the turntable detail. In the lower picture the shed's repair shop is seen, with its overhead gantry crane, powered through a superb collection of gear wheels. In the background is the often lethal line-shafting, with various belts for driving machine tools. With typical Victorian sternness and love of decoration, the repair shop is not only provided with doors, to stop thievery, but those doors are topped by spikes; they are then beautified by the fitting of finials atop the door posts! In a short while all this would come crashing down, to be lost forever.

W. Potter

Plates 166 to 168: There was another shed at Neath — the Neath & Brecon Railway depot at Bridge Street, which saw some change over the years. In the upper picture, dating from 2nd June 1926, we see, according to the official GWR photographic negative catalogue, the *original* N&B shed. It certainly looks like a shed and there was some mention in the N&B's archives about a new shed being required, from 1887, 23 years after the railway opened. Quite honestly, the author doesn't know, so it is left for the reader to make up his own mind. In the undated centre view is the building which faced that shown above, and possibly was built about 1887. The two-road carriage shed on the right was demolished during the 1930s, leaving the remainder to see out World War II, by which time its condition was desperate. Accordingly, it was replaced in 1946 by the brick and concrete structure seen below — destined to be the very last engine shed to be erected by the GWR. Locomotives visible are Nos 5778, 3621 and 9734, and the date was 7th June 1953, eleven years before the shed closed. Such a modern building was bound to survive and so it does today, in private occupation.
BR/OPC, Author's Collection & B. Hilton

Plate 169: When this picture was taken, on 21st October 1979, this building at Newport (Dock Street) had seen nine years use as a loco shed and fifty years as a wagon shop! Replacing an 1854 Monmouthshire Railway shed that stood on the same site, Dock Street opened in 1920 and closed, surplus to requirements, in 1929; during its time as a shed it had an allocation of about forty locomotives. The building on the right was formerly part of the earlier shed.

J.A. Sommerfield

Plate 170: Newport (Ebbw Junction) Depot was a Churchward double turntable shed, the last to be built during his tenure as Chief Locomotive Engineer. It opened in 1915, replacing a cramped 1854 South Wales Railway shed at Newport (High Street). Initially known as Newport (Maesglas), Ebbw Junction featured, as may be seen, a large repair shop, a la Old Oak Common. With an allocation of around 150 engines for most of its existence, the shed presented a fantastic vista on Sundays, with line upon line of locomotives in the yard. This picture dates from 16th July 1952, which was a Wednesday!

B. Hilton

Plate 171: On opening, Ebbw Junction's repair shop was partly used for the manufacture of munitions. But, when this picture was taken, on 16th July 1952, all purposes were peaceful, with the roof supports framing six of the engines receiving attention.

B. Hilton

Plate 172: An 0-6-0PT, No. 3747, sits inside Newport (Ebbw Junction) Shed on 30th August 1964, in a picture included because of the somewhat unusual plates hung on the distant door. Quite what Metropolitan Railway destination boards were doing in South Wales is hard to say, and one wonders what untold tale lies behind them being so far from their London Transport origins.

K. Fairey

Plate 173: Proof positive that in dereliction, beauty may sometimes be found! The interior of Ebbw Junction Shed on 19th November 1967, 25 months after closure, with the rays of the winter sun softening the wrecker's handiwork.

J.A. Sommerfield

Plate 174: Newport's transporter bridge towers in the background of this classic South Wales shed view. It is a Sunday (21st August 1955) and virtually all the allocation of Newport (Pill) is at home, with non-vacuum fitted Class 6700 Pannier tanks predominating. This two-road depot was opened in 1898 by the Alexandra (Newport & South Wales) Dock & Railway Company, to succeed an 1875 shed, situated nearby. The GWR took over, extended the building, added the wooden coal stage seen on the right, and called the shed 'West Mendalgief' for a time. From the late 1950s, diesels progressively replaced steam on shunting duties, leading to the depot's closure in June 1963.

W. Potter

Plate 175: Ex-ADR 0-6-0T No. 667 stands beside Newport (Pill) Shed in the early 1950s. The 'northlight' roof detail is clearly seen and modellers may wish to note (and wonder at?) the six stepped layers of brickwork that buttress the roof's side walls.

W. Potter

Plates 176 & 177: There were two sheds at Newton Abbot during steam days. The first, of South Devon Railway origin, stood from December 1846 to November 1893, being succeeded by the depot seen here, a Dean 'northlight' shed. With the 20th century growth of holiday traffic, summer Saturdays at Newton Abbot could probably rival the GWR's busiest depots for activity. Trains carrying thousands of holiday-makers were constantly changing engines and taking bankers on and off. But, it was an awkward shed to watch, being tucked away behind sidings and, in the author's experience, a difficult one to 'bunk'. The photograph above shows the shed on a gloomy 16th April 1950, when some of the engines present were Nos 4405, 1362, 77000, 1018 *County of Leicester*, 5011 *Tintagel Castle*, 7220 and 6934 *Beachamwell Hall*. To illustrate the point about the shed's obscured view, the bottom picture shows the coaling stage from the station platform, on 3rd August 1948. Unusually, the intervening sidings are clear so No. 5108 and one 4-6-0 can be identified, but not so the locomotives taking coal, with wagons tantalizingly hiding their numbers! Note the wartime extension to the coal stage, the slaker in action just behind the 2-6-2T's chimney, and the water level indicator showing the 47,000 gallon tank to be about half full. All this detail came to an end with the shed's closure, in June 1962. The depot walls still stand today, but must surely now have a limited future.

C.H.S. Owen & W. Potter

Plates 178 to 180: Neyland was one of the few broad gauge sheds to survive change and its mixed 2-road/1-road layout had an interesting history. Opened in 1856 by the South Wales Railway, the original portion comprised the re-erected one-time loco shed from Chepstow (West), where it had stood from 1850 to 1854/5. After a time, this building became insufficient for Neyland's allocation, so a second portion was added, at a date unknown, to form the shed that did not close until December 1963. In the top picture, the one-road northern end is seen, on 20th September 1962, with one of Neyland's elusive 'County' class locomotives inside. On the right is the 65ft. turntable and water tank, on top of its lofty pumphouse; the coal stage is out of view, on the left. The centre, 1930s' picture, shows the two-road southern end, with offices along the west wall, the sand house at the shed entrance and some interesting rolling stock. Below, Carmarthen's 'Dean Goods', No. 2411, is seen during April 1947. She stands at the point where the two buildings join, leading to speculation as to which was the shed that once stood at Chepstow. The author favours the single-road section.
W.T. Stubbs Collection, B. Matthews Collection & W. Potter

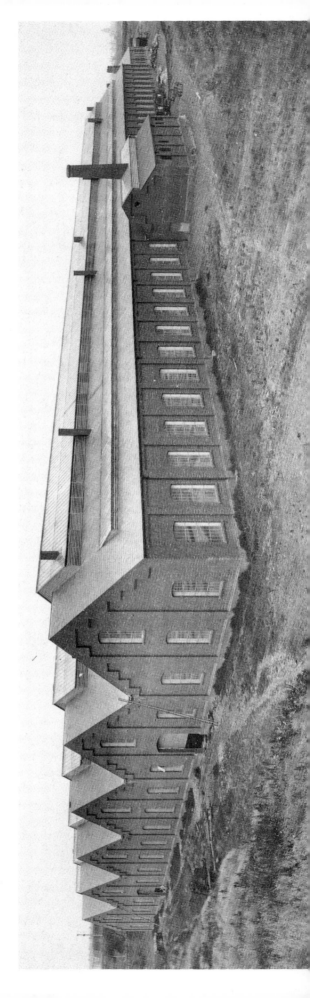

Plates 181 & 182: By far the greatest of the GWR's engine sheds, in every way, Old Oak Common's massive quadruple turntable depot opened in 1906. Built to Churchward's design, it provided the prototype standard for all succeeding turntable sheds, and must be considered to have been very successful, in all aspects. It would be difficult to encompass such a large building in a single photograph, but these two views, taken during the late construction period, give some idea of its size — something only approached by a few of the North Eastern Railway's turntable sheds.

BR/OPC

Plates 183 & 184: Old Oak Common through the ages, with the view above showing the South Yard soon after the shed's opening, containing a superb collection of 4-4-0s and a Single. In the far distance, a 'County' is about to pass the entrance to the south-east turntable. From a similar vantage point (below), on 3rd July 1963, we see a forest of lighting posts with, by the same measure, a modest 'glade' of water cranes, and a host of four men to water a Large Prairie. Left of centre is the BR-built office block and left of that, the standby locomotive — invariably a 'Castle' as on that day. Left again is the Ransomes & Rapier 45 ton steam breakdown crane, No. 16, delivered to Old Oak Common in 1940, only leaving in 1972 for Saltley. When last seen, in October 1984, Crane No. 16 was lying at Swindon, out of use.

B. Matthews Collection & W.T. Stubbs Collection

Plate 185. Old Oak Common's massive 104ft. ×60ft. double-sided coal stage, with ten tips, and topped by a 290,000 gallon tank, is seen here, around opening. In typically immaculate condition, graceful Atlantic No. 190 and Class 2201 No. 2206, were obviously specially posed for the official photographer, complete with their somewhat self-conscious looking crews!

BR/OPC

Plate 186: Another Old Oak Common yard scene, with the picture, at top, featuring the solitary GWR Pacific, No. 111 *The Great Bear*. It is 8th April 1922 and she sits forlornly contemplating her future, which will not be much, as she was withdrawn in January 1924. Just visible is Old Oak's large repair shop — probably where No. 111's tender was receiving attention.

W. Potter

Plate 187: With four turntables under one roof, Churchward wisely incorporated side entrances, so that all turntables had a separate access. Here is No. 4705, on 15th May 1938, parked by the side entrance leading to the north-west turntable.

W. Potter

Plates 188 & 189: The interior of Old Oak Common Shed was too much for one photograph to contain. The top picture, taken on 8th April 1922, shows a few stabling roads of the north-east turntable (traditionally the tank engine turntable), cabless 'Metro' tank No. 3586, and a nearby 'Star'. Yet it manages to convey something of the awesome scope of the place, as it dwindles away into a smoky distance. A slightly better impression of depth is gained below, in a picture taken in August 1960, from the south-west turntable. The sunlight streaming through the side entrance catches the wheels of No. 1007 *County of Brecknock*. Also seen are Nos. 6917 *Oldlands Hall* and 6029 *King Edward VIII*, the latter temporarily out of traffic, as seen by the 'NOT TO BE MOVED' plate.

W. Potter & T. Wright

Plates 190 & 191: Naturally, Old Oak Common was supplied with a breakdown train and hosted many different steam cranes in its time. The last, 45 ton No. 16, is distantly seen in *Plate 184*, while these pictures show two of its antecedents. Above, seen inside the shed about 1910, is Crane No. 7, of 15 tons capacity and built by Cowans Sheldon in 1901. Originally numbered '1', this crane became No. 7 about 1909, when a 36 ton crane, from the Bath-based company of Stothert & Pitt, came to Old Oak Common and was designated No. 1. No. 7 eventually found its way to Oswestry, and then Swindon, where it ended its days in 1956. The Stothert & Pitt machine's presence was obviously somewhat tenuous in the early 1900s, as 12 ton crane No. 12 was at Old Oak Common around 1910, while in the lower picture is seen Crane No. 5 in 1912, posed with a match wagon and Old Oak Common riding van. No. 5 was of 20 tons capacity and came from Cowans Sheldon in 1903. After some time at Old Oak, No. 5 went to Swindon, from where it was withdrawn in 1965.

P. Tatlow Collection & British Rail

Plate 192: The headquarters of the Cambrian Railways, Oswestry, was the location of the company's main works and loco shed, which opened in 1860. The shed is seen here at an unknown date, but probably around the turn of the century, with two Cambrian 4-4-0s parked outside. The depot's 4 roads/2 roads layout strongly suggests that it had been extended at some time (by two roads?), although no record of such an expansion has yet been found.
B. Matthews Collection

Plate 193: Oswestry's low-pitched hipped roofs lasted well, but eventually they had to be replaced. Such work was in progress on 9th July 1950, when a typically mixed bag of residents was on display.
B. Hilton

Plate 194: One year and ten days later, the new steel and asbestos roof had been finished, this covering surviving until the shed closed in January 1965. The GWR provided the coal stage and a 45,000 gallon tank in 1929, and these are seen together with the 60ft. turntable, with No. 7823 *Hook Norton Manor* aboard. Some of the other engines seen are: Nos 9026, 1604, 7819 *Hinton Manor*, 2244 and 3208. After closure the shed was taken over for industrial purposes, which continues today.
W. Potter

Plate 195: Oxford was reached by the GWR in 1850 and the first shed opened in July of that year. Four years later the OW&WR started operations from Oxford, and built a shed diagonally opposite the GWR depot, across the intervening River Isis. In 1863 the ailing OW&WR was taken over by the GWR which, for the next 13 years or so, operated both loco sheds. However, around 1876, the GWR building became a carriage shed and all locomotive activities were concentrated at the OW&WR depot. That shed is shown above on 2nd August 1954, in a scene that epitomises Oxford's cosmopolitan situation, as one of the very few places where locomotives of all four pre-nationalisation companies, and four BR regions, could be observed. D16/3 class locomotive No. 62585 is backing off shed to pick up its train for Cambridge, a late lamented cross-country service.

E.V. Fry

Plate 196: 'Metro'tank No. 3562 simmers in the yard at Oxford on 3rd July 1948. In the background is the ex-LNWR shed at Rewley Road, with what looks like 2P No. 455 in residence. The LNWR shed did not last much longer, being closed on 3rd December 1950, leaving the one-time OW&WR broad gauge building to see out the days of steam, and close in January 1967, in near original condition, after almost 113 years of service.

W. Potter

Plate 197: With winter precipitation causing the River Thames to burst its banks, 'Single' No. 1125, then some 30 years old, poses on Oxford's brand-new 65ft. turntable, on 11th January 1906. As may be seen, the turntable was supplied by the well-known Ipswich firm of Ransomes & Rapier. Later, the centre access road would become a short dead-end spur, when a ramp coaling stage was erected immediately behind where the camera stood.

BR/OPC

Plates 198 to 200: Oxley's double-turntable shed was opened in 1907, to relieve serious congestion at Wolverhampton (Stafford Road) Depot. Because of site restrictions, the turntables were arranged longitudinally — the only depot to have this layout. However, like all the Churchward twin-turntable sheds, Oxley's coal and water facilities were provided with an eye to future expansion, as the site could accommodate four turntables, albeit after such expensive preparation. Not surprisingly, the shed was never enlarged, so it closed in near original state in March 1967. The top picture shows Oxley's No. 5919 *Worsley Hall* and three generations of heavy freight locomotives standing outside the depot in 1960. Thirty eight years earlier (centre), pre-grouping pride! A commendably clean Oxley Shed interior and an equally smart 'Beyer Goods' No. 353 are seen together on 26th August 1922. By June 1938 (bottom), Oxley's repair shop still had a clean, if cluttered, interior, but locomotive cleanliness had deteriorated, if the unidentified half-cab Pannier tank is anything to go by.

S. Rickard & W. Potter (2)

Plate 201: Pantyfynnon was provided with a four-road 'Loans Act' shed in March 1931, enabling closure of the 91 year old Llanelly Railway shed at Garnant. With all the usual facilities, except a repair shop, Pantyfynnon normally had an allocation of some 16 locomotives for working services over the lines from Llanelly to Llandilo, Garnant and Cross Hands. It is seen here in 1936, in 'as new' condition, with a single 2-8-0T in residence. Closure was in August 1964, with subsequent demolition, but Pantyfynnon remains a diesel stabling point.
B Matthews

Plate 202: Destined to serve for 100 years, Pembroke Dock Shed was opened by the Pembroke & Tenby Railway in 1863, to be absorbed by the GWR in 1897. Depicted here, on 18th April 1954, the stone-built depot shows evidence of re-roofing; the 1900 rear extension, in wood, is also just visible. No. 4132 takes it easy before returning to Whitland.
E.V. Fry

Plates 203 & 204: Before the Grouping, the Great Western and Cambrian Railways made an end-on junction at Dolgelly, to provide a through route from Ruabon to Barmouth. In 1869, the Cambrian built a shed at Penmaenpool, the nearest convenient point to their railhead. That attractive little building is seen above on 10th August 1958, with its inmates having just been logged by the departing enthusiasts. Notice how even after so many years, the former divisional working has been maintained. No. 6303 is from the ex-GWR parent shed of Croes Newydd, while No. 5801 is from Machynlleth, representing old Cambrian interests. Notice too the wealth of detail, with coal platform, piles of ash, numerous shovels scattered around, fire irons neatly stacked and even fire buckets each side of the entrance. Further detail is visible in the picture below, taken in 1964, which shows that, although motive power changed over the years, old GW/Cambrian divisions did not with Nos 75029 and 46521 representing Croes Newydd and Machynlleth, respectively. Penmaenpool Shed closed in January of the next year but, by extraordinary coincidence, both locomotives survived the holocaust, with No. 75029 today residing at Cranmore and No. 46521 working on the Severn Valley Railway.

W. Potter & C.L. Caddy

Plate 205: Penzance's third and last steam loco shed, at Long Rock, just after completion in January 1914. See how the ground has been built up to accommodate the building, and also the interesting contactor's stationary engine between the shed and turntable. This Churchward standard depot had replaced a nearby two-road 1876 building which incorporated the earlier West Cornwall Railway shed in its layout. Long Rock served the cause of steam until September 1962, after which it housed diesels, only closing when the HST depot was opened a few years ago.

British Rail

Plate 206: An obscure depot, the little shed in Plymouth Docks, seen here on 25th September 1961, is thought to have been built during the late 1860s to house the shunting engines working this large seaport. Millbay Shed was nearby, but presumably the GWR considered the expense worthwhile to save light engine movements. Precious little else is known — even the closing date is uncertain — thought to have been around the mid-1950s.

W.T. Stubbs Collection

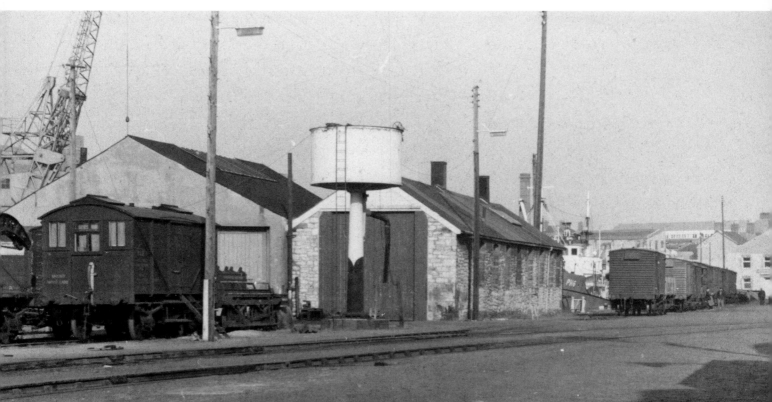

Plate 207: In dire need of a coat of paint, the shed at Pontrilas was at the southern end of the former Golden Valley Railway's route from Clifford. The GWR absorbed that impoverished little concern in 1901 and built this shed in the same year, to replace the 1881 GVR depot that had, coincidentally, just burned down! The picture dates from 14th September 1952, when 0-4-2T No. 5819 was inside. Assuredly, British Railways did not apply the much-needed paint, as the depot closed four and a half months later.

W. Potter

Plate 208: A 'what became of the shed after closure' picture with a difference. Pontypool (Crane Street) in September 1936, with a Pannier officiating on pilot duty E13; the station forecourt is at the bottom right. A study of contemporary maps shows that between 1854 and 1878 a one-road Monmouthshire Railway shed had stood on the site occupied by allotments, immediately above the forecourt. Crane Street goods yard closed, incidentally, on 28th June 1965.

W. Potter

Plates 209 & 210: The Great Western's second turntable shed, Pontypool Road opened in 1865. It was extended only four years later, on its southern side, by the addition of an eight-road straight shed, with one internal road connecting both buildings. The entrance to the turntable shed is seen in the top view, on 14th September 1952. The electrician's mate, dutifully 'footing' the ladder, watches with interest as a Large Prairie makes a smoky exit. Inside Pontypool turntable shed in September 1936 (below), the stone walls and original wooden roof boards were clearly visible. Notice also the U-section rails on the stabling roads — almost certainly as installed in 1865. There must have been some 'esprit de corps' at the depot in those days, half a century ago, as No. 1600 and her nearby sister were obviously well cared for.

W. Potter

Plates 211 & 212: Spot the difference! The southern end of Pontypool Road's 1869 straight shed, in pictures taken 27 years apart. In September 1936 (above), the shed was nearly empty and the goods yard was visible on the left. By 1963 (below), the shed had lost its doors, and the wood and tile roof had been superseded by corrugated asbestos, with large ventilators along the ridges. The sand furnace had lost its chimney and there is ash dumped in the yard. Lastly, and most obvious, it is a Sunday, so the goods yard is obscured by locomotives cramming the shed — and yes, there is a group of enthusiasts on a visit!

W. Potter & C.L. Caddy

Plate 213: A close-up of Pontypool Road's re-roofed straight shed on 12th October 1958. A brace of 2-8-2Ts and a pair of Panniers pose in the late afternoon sunshine, while a diesel shunter intrudes. This large depot closed after 100 years, in May 1965, and today's desolate wasteland, with a new road cutting through it, is all that remains of the shed and the extensive yards it once served.

T.W. Nicholls

Plate 214: Back to September 1936 again, and Pontypool Road's coal stage, sited north of the turntable shed, displays its three tips and rake of 'Loco' coal wagons on the brick-piered extension track. The GWR installed the stage in 1898, giving it a pitched roof, as the shed already had a 60,000 gallon water tank, on top of the original coal stage *(see Plate 210)*. The small louvre-walled building was a sand house.

W. Potter

Plate 215: The Cambrian Railways' shed at Portmadoc, on 6th July 1958. It had been built in 1907 to replace a 40 year old single-road shed on the same site. Locomotives on shed that day were Nos 2202, 2233, 2280, 4560, 5517, 9013 and 78006. It is difficult to envisage nowadays, that there was sufficient traffic to provide employment for all that power, on what was basically, a single-track secondary main line. Eventually the traffic and locomotives faded away, and the shed closed in August 1963.

B. Hilton

Plate 216: At some 1,350ft. up, on the side of Dartmoor, Princetown probably had the highest situated loco shed in England. Opened in 1883, when the Princetown Railway completed its tortuous line from Yelverton, the shed was of classic GWR outline, with a 5,500 gallon tank over the entrance, a small coal platform, and miniscule turntable, all seen here in a late 1940s picture. For many years Class 4400 2-6-2Ts were exclusive power for this difficult route, until its closure, in March 1956.

Woodfin Collection, Courtesy of Bristol City Museum

Plates 217 & 218: The Cambrian Railways' terminus at Pwllheli had three sheds over the years. The first stood from October 1867, until 1907, when it was replaced by the depot seen above, coincident with the opening of a new station. This undated picture shows an extraordinarily long building, which is not surprising, as previously it had served as a carriage shed at the original station — probably dating back to 1867, therefore. Needless to say, a wooden structure of such age eventually had to be replaced, but not until 1958, when British Railways put up the GWR system's last ever steam shed. That two-road depot is seen below, in the early 1960s, with a Class 2251 0-6-0 and BR Class 4 4-6-0 in attendance — the latter being the last type of locomotive to use the shed before closure, in 1966. Note the conveyor for coaling and fire irons neatly encircled by a length of hosepipe. The BR-built shed still stands in industrial use.

Author's Collection & J. Hooper Collection

Plates 219 to 221: Clydach Vale Colliery's output was sufficient to cause both the GWR and TVR to build mineral branches to extract the 'black diamonds'. The former used a heavily graded extension of the branch from Llantrisant to Pen-y-Graig, while the TVR resorted to a cable incline from Tonypandy, on the Porth to Treherbert line. The Pwllyrhebog Incline had a shed at the summit, which housed the three Class H 0-6-0T locomotives that shunted the sidings. Normally only one or two H Class were at Pwllyrhebog, with the remainder being at the main shed of Treherbert, for routine maintenance. The top picture shows the shed on 14th October 1949, with No. 195 as the resident shunter. In the background is the GWR line, with two Pannier tanks struggling up the grade from Blaenclydach, with empties for the colliery. The centre picture is not a shed, but it shows the Pwllrhebog incline at work, on 4th May 1951, two months before operations ceased. The standard method of changing over engines is seen, with No. 195 going up, pushing empties, to take over shunting duties from No. 196, coming down in the distance. In the bottom view, No. 195 is again seen, in store at Treherbert on 8th August 1951; the cable-gripping gear is clearly visible.

W. Potter (top & bottom) &
H.C. Casserley (centre)

Plate 222: A silvan setting for Radstock Shed in 1975, no less than 46 years after closure, and serving as a garage and store for the adjacent privately-owned wagon works. Opened in 1866, the depot housed locomotives for shunting, trips and local passenger trains in this part of the once prolific, but now totally defunct, Somerset coalfield.
Author

Plate 223: Count the locomotives — the author sees at least 23! The famous South Wales Sunday scene at Radyr, on 12th July 1959. Obviously a 'Loan Act' building, the shed opened on 29th March 1931, replacing a 66 year old TVR depot that stood on a site behind the camera. For much of its life a sub-shed of Cardiff (Cathays), Radyr gained main shed status, and shed code 88A, in December 1957. Closure was in July 1965, since when the Civil Engineer has used the building, and diesel locomotives continue to stable in the surrounding yards.
T.J. Edgington

Plate 224: The GWR's most famous stabling point, normally busier than many of its loco sheds. Ranelagh Road, just outside Paddington, is seen soon after nationalisation, with thirteen locomotives present; three 2-6-2T, five 'Castles' (one an oil-burner), one 'King', three 'Halls' and one 'Star' — the latter on the extreme right, as standby locomotive. The turntable and water tank were removed after the end of steam, but Ranelagh Road continued to stable diesels, until rendered unnecessary by the introduction of HSTs.
OPC

Plate 225: Ex-MSWJ 2-4-0 No. 1336 looks across the largely roofless turntable shed at Reading on 23rd August 1930, seeing a 'Star' and an 'Aberare'' in the eastern shed yard. Sited in the triangle of lines west of Reading (General) Station, this depot had opened in 1880, succeeding an 1840 two-road broad gauge shed opposite the station. Almost immediately after this picture was taken, work commenced on a conversion unique in GWR history — the turntable shed became a nine road straight shed.

H.C. Casserley

Plates 226 & 227: Reading as a straight shed, seen from the east, in the photograph above, on 31st August 1945, with the 1932 repair shop on the right. Note the LMS 0-6-0, one of a number of other railways' locomotives that were 'hostilities only' draftees to the GWR, to cover the absence of 'Dean Goods', away on WD service. Below, the western and is depicted on 10th August 1951, with the 65ft. turntable giving No. 5075 *Wellington* a new direction in life! Later the turntable was to lose its boarded covering and gain guard rails around the open pit; also to disappear was the railmotor shed visible behind the 'Castle's' tender. In the left-hand section of the building Mogul No. 6366 can just be seen, and left of that is Railcar No. 33, one of the five or six allocated to Reading at the time.

BR/OPC & L. B. Lapper courtesy N.E. Preedy

Plate 228: Forming a backdrop to Armstrong 'Standard Goods' No. 1196 is Reading's coal stage, on 18th February 1922. The stage stood in the western yard and, as may be noticed, did not have the customary tank on the roof. Instead, two tanks stood on their own supports by the south-west corner of the shed; these may be seen in *Plate 226.*

W. Potter

Plate 229: No. 118 was typical of the small steam cranes that used to serve the coaling and ash disposal duties at most of the GWR's loco sheds. Of about one to two tons capacity, it is depicted here in Reading Shed's coal yard, around 1950. Unfortunately the author is not aware of the crane's manufacturers, or the date of building.

P. Tatlow Collection

Plates 230 & 231: The northern terminus of the Rhymney Railway at Rhymney, in two scenes, dating from 25th August 1935 and 6th July 1952. The former (above) shows the shed as built in the early 1860s, with stone walls and wooden roof. Pannier tank No. 5769 is nearest the camera, and in the station a train prepares to depart northwards, over the RR/LNWR Joint line, towards Nantybwch. By 1952 (centre), the shed had been re-roofed and a signal box had appeared by the south-eastern corner. The coal stage on the left is looking a little care-worn, and would soon be replaced by a gantry coaler. The 0-6-2T locomotives, Nos 80 and 370, had only a few years left, but the depot did not close until March 1965, when over a century old.

B. Matthews & W. Potter

Plate 232: Ross-on-Wye was the junction of the lines from Gloucester (via Grange Court) and Monmouth, to Hereford. Opened in 1855 as a broad gauge depot, the stone-built shed stood in the fork of the lines and was destined to serve until October 1963. Not without alteration however, as this June 1956 photograph shows that the shed had been re-roofed in brick at some time. However the original broad gauge arched lintel was faithfully copied, even though the entrance had been reduced to 'narrow gauge Gothic' many years before. When the author visited the site in 1975, the shed still stood, rapidly being obscured by surrounding trees. Since then it has found other use, as an antique shop.

A.R. Goult

Plates 233 & 234: With a design of building unusual among GWR sheds, St. Blazey's part-roundhouse was opened by the Cornwall Minerals Railway in 1872, to be absorbed by the GWR in 1896. Serving china clay and, eventually, holiday industries, the depot operated a network of Cornish branch lines and had a number of sub-sheds. These two views, from 25th August 1959, show (above) eight of the shed's nine covered roads; note that the turntable has been vacuum-fitted. No. 4547 (below) under repair, is framed by the hoist, and a Pannier tank, 'Hall' and an ancient crane sit in front of the CME's workshops. Closed to steam in April 1962, St. Blazey remains an operational depot, still serving china clay interests and the branch to the popular resort of Newquay. Classified a 'Listed Building', of significant architectural/historical interest, although the building is being considered for closure during 1987.

K. Fairey

Plate 235: Taken from a commercial postcard bearing a 1912 postmark, but probably much older than that, is this view of Porthminster (St. Ives) with the 1877-built loco shed in the centre. Much later on, the distant hillside would be covered by hotels and houses, and the distant beach would be covered by holiday-makers and hippies! Note the scores of fishing boats, at that time St. Ives' major source of livelihood.

B. Hilton Collection

Plate 236: A July 1957 close-up of St. Ives Shed, showing No. 4540 resting, before returning to St. Erth. The coal platform is seen between the supports of the 10,000 gallon water tank, while on the right is a recently added relay cabin. The shed closed in September 1961.

B. Hilton

Plate 237. Severn Tunnel Junction, a Churchward four-road depot, seen soon after opening in 1907. It had superseded an 1886 two-road shed by the station which, however, saw a further 20 years use as a railmotor depot. Witness the land-filling that was necessary to support the new shed and yard, and the immaculate condition of the locomotives. The turntable is behind the building and a 42,000 gallon tank tops the coal stage.

BR/OPC

Plate 238: Further land-filling enabled a two-road extension at Severn Tunnel Junction to be completed in 1939. It is seen here on 23rd September 1961, with a glimpse of the locomotive sidings that were laid beside it. Visible behind the shed is the standard repair shop, added in the early 1940s. The depot closed in October 1965, and afterwards found further use as a terminal for the Ford Motor Company's car-carrier trains. It has since been demolished.

W.T. Stubbs Collection

Plates 239 & 240: Severn Tunnel Junction was the location of one of the GWR's locomen's hostels, used by crews working lodging turns. Quite often such hostels were sited in the dirtiest, noisiest places, close to, or even within, loco shed environs. This ensured that staff were conveniently close, but conversely, it also ensured they didn't get much rest! At Severn Tunnel Junction, however, the hostel was far enough away from the loco shed to ensure it could at least be kept clean. This may be appreciated from the section of the dormitory area, seen at left (below) showing the fairly primitive wooden partitioning that made up the individual sleeping cubicles. Each cubicle contained a frame bed, perhaps a small locker, and a hook or two, for hanging clothes. Apart from beds and basic washing facilities, a kitchen was provided so that the men could prepare their own food whilst stopping over. That kitchen is depicted here (below, right) note the large coal-fired range, with its associated hot water tank — both very stoutly made in cast iron. These photographs date from November 1919, when, as may be seen, the hostel's lighting was still being provided by unprotected gas mantles. The practice of working socially unacceptable lodging turns was much reduced from the early BR period, so the need for establishments like locomen's dormitories gradually faded away.

BR/OPC

Plates 241 & 242: Shrewsbury (Coleham's) sprawling buildings were a legacy of its GWR/LNWR Joint operation, with both companies using the 1855 Shrewsbury & Hereford Railway shed, in addition to their own separate premises at Coton Hill (GWR) and Abbey Foregate (LNWR). However, in 1877, the LNWR opened a ten-road depot beside the S&H shed, leaving the GWR to fully occupy and progressively expand the old buildings, closing its four-road Coton Hill shed meanwhile. In the top picture, all the Coleham buildings are seen, on 11th June 1961, with the former GWR 'side' on the left and the ex-LMS 'side' on the right, with an S&H office building forming a link. Note the separate coaling facilities still in use — a GWR coal stage, topped by a 33,000 gallon tank, and an LNWR coaling shed. The whole complex was under Western Region control in 1961, becoming a Midland Region responsibility in 1963, to be finally closed on 6th November 1967. The bottom picture shows a rather smoky GWR side in the early 1960s. The right-hand two buildings were the original S&H shed, subdivided internally by a wall, into two-road and three-road sections, with the GWR keeping strictly to the former and the LNWR, the latter. Soon after gaining all five roads of the straight shed, the GWR found itself short of space, so in 1886, a single turntable shed was built at the rear (unseen in this picture). With its rear wall removed, the three-road portion of the straight shed gave access to the turntable, with all three tracks running on to it: at the same time, the two-road section became a repair shop. There matters rested until 1932, when the three-road 'Loans Act' shed, seen on the left, appeared on the site of an old wagon shop. All these buildings remained in gradually dwindling use until the end.

W. Potter & W.T. Stubbs

Plate 243: In March 1936, ROD 2-8-0 No. 3023 simmers in the entrance of the three-road shed, beside the coal stack dividing Shrewsbury's GWR and LMS sections. Although all three roads led to the turntable, only the centre one was usually used for access, with locomotives stabling on the other two.

W. Potter

Plate 244: The interior of Shrewsbury's turntable shed, the first to have a Dean 'northlight' roof, on 21st June 1947, with a weary looking 4-4-0, No. 9076 on view. Note the method of roof construction — with low headroom lattice girders and wooden roof boards and an absence of smoke ducts over each stabling road.

H.C. Casserley

Plate 245: No servicing facilities were provided at the small shed at Shipston-on-Stour, from its opening in 1889. This omission seemed to characterise the shed's lack of importance, and it is not surprising that closure came after only a relatively short time, in 1916. There then followed two years in military use before the building became a garage. It was still in very good condition on 31st August 1952, when it was photographed during an RCTS railtour over the branch from Moreton-in-Marsh.

T.J. Edgington

Plates 246 & 247: Slough's original 1840 loco shed was replaced in 1868. Replacement was done on the cheap, by converting the existing Windsor line goods shed into a two road locomotive depot, and adding another two-road bay. This brick-walled, tiled-roof building is seen (centre) in 1934, doubtless on a Sunday, to judge by the number of engines present. Later, it would be re-roofed in asbestos with brick gable ends, and it is seen in that condition, below, from the other end, on 12th May 1962. Slough loco shed closed in June 1964, when all surviving locomotives were moved to Southall.

D.K. Jones & T. Wright

Plates 248 & 249:   Southall gained its first engine shed in 1859, when the Great Western & Brentford Railway opened a one-road building for housing locomotives working the branch to the Thames-side at Brentford. The GW&BR depot was superseded in 1884 by the second of Dean's six-road 'northlight' sheds, and this is seen above, relatively unchanged, about 1932. The twin stationary boilers and repair shop are noteworthy, as is the absence of any water cranes from their usual position outside the shed; a water point was situated by the coal stage, which stood behind the camera. By the very dawn of BR (below), in a view from the coal stage, the shed had lost its 'northlight' roof in favour of a very rudimentary covering — probably as a result of wartime depredations. This covering survived until 1953 when BR demolished the entire shed and replaced it with the structure seen in the next photograph.

Author's Collection

Plate 250: BR's modern shed at Southall opened in 1954. As this 25th September 1963 picture shows, it was built in steel and corrugated materials, covering eight roads, with the two northernmost (left, in the picture) allocated for diesel power from the outset. A large repair shop, skip hoist coaling plant and 65ft. turntable, all sited in the rear yard, completed the facilities. Notice that water cranes are provided in the locomotive yard. Southall became London's last outpost for Western steam, until December 1965, when it was finally banished; diesels continued to use the shed until final closure in November 1986. Miraculously, Southall is now serving steam locomotives again, since the building was leased by Mr. W. McAlpine, for use as the London base for engines working the highly successful SLOA/BR Sunday luncheon specials from Marylebone.

W.T. Stubbs

Plate 251: Southall used railmotors for longer than any other GWR depot — April 1904 to May 1935. They worked such services as Southall— Brentford, Southall— Perivale— Westbourne Park, Westbourne Park— West Ealing— Perivale— Ruislip, West Drayton— Staines and Uxbridge (Vine Street), Gerards Cross— Uxbridge (High Street) and Park Royal— Willesden Junction. A single-road railmotor shed was erected at Southall in 1905; it is partially visible on the right of this photograph, dating from 20th May 1933, showing 5ft. 2in. Pannier tank No. 5419 sandwiched between two auto-coaches. The main 'northlight' depot is also just seen, between the rear coach and the railmotor shed.

W. Potter

Plates 252 & 253: Stourbridge Junction's 1970 four-road depot was formally closed on 8th February 1926, when the last of all the GWR's turntable sheds — a Churchward style single unit — opened on an adjacent site. However, the old building continued in use, for railmotors, as may be seen from the view above, which dates from 24th April 1932. Wartime pressures caused the shed to be officially reopened in 1944, eventually to pass to BR, be re-roofed, and not finally close until July 1965, when the turntable shed too went out of use. The bottom picture shows the refurbished shed on 14th June 1953, with Nos 2824, 3821 and Railcars Nos 8 and 33 in residence.

W. Potter & B. Hilton

Plates 254 & 255: A panoramic view, photographed on 13th March 1960, of Stourbridge Junction, showing the relative positions of the 1870 and 1926 buildings. The former is now squarely the diesel shed, with Railcars Nos 15 and 8 having been ousted by BR 'buses'. There seems to be plenty of activity at the turntable shed, to judge by the smoke and number of locomotives lying around the yard. Like a lot of GWR sheds, Stourbridge's coal stage was extended during World War II, to allow both-sides coaling, and this extension is clearly seen on the left-hand side; the tank held 75,000 gallons. In the lower picture, the turntable shed is seen in close-up, on 22nd April 1962, with Nos 7907 *Hart Hall*, 48424 and 48475. The 8Fs were Swindon-built, and had been allocated to Western Region sheds for some years. After closure, both sheds were demolished and a housing estate now covers their sites.

W Potter & W.T. Stubbs

Plate 256: Stratford-upon-Avon's two-road Churchward depot, on 8th September 1957, with the town's gasworks behind. No. 3847 is in steam, while No. 43873 and her two LMS 0-6-0 sisters seem to be out of use. The LMS types had appeared at the GWR depot two months before, when Stratford's ex-SMJR shed closed. The GWR depot dated from 1910, having replaced an 1859 OW&W building sited elsewhere; closure was in September 1962.

A.R. Goult

Plate 257: Swansea's docks were the location of no less than eight different sheds over the years. The majority of these were built by various contractors working the port complex, with a couple eventually coming into GWR ownership at the Grouping. However, previous to that, the GWR had its own three-road shed at Swansea East Dock which, while opened in 1893, differed from the then norm in having a single-pitched roof, instead of a 'northlight' style. It is seen below, in June 1935, with 0-4-0ST No. 935 and 0-6-2 tanks Nos. 5663 and 6681 awaiting Monday's return to duty. The shed closed in June 1964 and was demolished, but still, today, diesels stable near its site.

B. Hilton Collection

Plates 258 & 259: Following closure of the original broad gauge depot in the works complex, Swindon's second shed grew in two stages. First was the 1871 nine-road straight shed, which had a single turntable unit at the rear, five internal roads connected the two sections, all under one roof, which had three longitudinal pitches and glazed ends. The second stage occurred in 1908, when Churchward added one of his turntable units, which adjoined the earlier shed on its eastern side; there was no internal rail connection between the old and new buildings. These two pictures show the southern end of the depot. Above, on 11th September 1932, shows (left to right) coal stage, nine-road 1871 shed and 1908 turntable shed. The time is late afternoon and a group of 1930s' enthusiasts are completing their visit. Below, 27 years and 16 days later, a close-up of the straight shed shows that the right-hand two roads have been given over to diesel shunters and the railbuses which worked the Cirencester and Tetbury branches. Apart from that, and a few Standard locomotives, little has changed.

B. Matthews & K. Fairey

Plate 260: By 9th May 1964, much had changed at Swindon from the previous picture! Diesels now ruled and former steam superstars were relegated to the enjoyable, but nonetheless artificial, duties of enthusiasts' railtour power — hence this scene. No. 46251 *City of Nottingham*, resplendent in maroon, is absolutely appropriate power (by request) for one of the famed RCTS 'East Midlander' tours; No. 46251 was soon to go to the breakers. A not quite so shiny No. 7022 *Hereford Castle* was present as Swindon's standby for the fantastic 'Great Western' railtour, which the author has already enthused over, in the caption to *Plate 44*. No. 7022's services were not required that day, and like No. 46251, the 'Castle' was soon to die under the Cutter's torch.

K. Fairey

Plates 261 & 262: Swindon interiors. At the top, the 1908 turntable shed in September 1938. Nos 2842, 2947 *Madresfield Court*, 2978 *Charles J Hambro* (formerly *Kirkland*) and 2945 *Hillingdon Court*, make a marvellous sight as they await their next duties. Note that No. 2945 differs from her sister 'Saints' in having outside steam pipes and a short safety-valve cover. Those superb gas lamps would eventually be replaced by electric types, but the manual turntables remained. The lagged pipe circling the turntable, behind the smoke ducts, carried heated water for washing out boilers. At the bottom, is a 1934 picture taken inside the 1871 turntable shed, which was used mostly by tank engines after the second turntable unit opened. No. 5801 sits on one of the radiating roads with, behind, some of the straight shed's terminating roads and, on the left, through roads to the turntable.

B. Hilton Collection & D.K. Jones

Plate 263: Steam Crane No. 12 was allocated to Swindon for most of its life, with one interlude at Old Oak Common. This machine was unique in two ways: firstly, it was the GWR's only 12 ton capacity crane, and secondly, it was the first and last crane ever provided to the GWR by J.H. Wilson & Company, of Sandhills, Liverpool, being manufactured in 1908. Weighing nearly 50 tons, and equipped with a 39ft. jib, it is portrayed here, just after delivery, at Swindon Works. The last recorded sighting of No. 12 was at Swindon, in October 1960; withdrawal came soon after that.

British Rail

Plates 264 & 265: Tucked away between the rear of Swindon's main loco shed and the gasworks, was the stock shed. Coming under workshop control, instead of the Running Department, this six-road 'northlight' building was erected around the early 1890s, to hold locomotives that were surplus to requirements or awaiting workshops attention. Seen above, on 10th May 1953, ex-MSWJ 2-4-0 No. 1336 pauses on its last journey to 'C' Shop; No. 5090 *Neath Abbey* waits the call to 'A' Shop, and an unidentified steam crane busies itself with some recovered track. Below, the late 1950s picture shows the standard lightweight construction of a 'northlight' roof, with a single central row of supporting columns, and the roof's weight between columns and side walls being taken by transverse tie rods. Locomotives seen are Nos 2516, 3101, 3100, 3102 and 1458.

B. Hilton & W. Potter

Plates 266 & 267: A Dean single turntable shed was provided at Taunton in 1896. It replaced a B&ER two-road depot that dated back to 1841, being first a temporary shed at Bridgwater, and then occupying two different sites at Taunton — 1842— 1860 and 1860— 1896. The 'northlight' roofed turntable shed is seen above, circa 1910, with the sand drier in the foreground. From a slightly more distant aspect (below) on 1st September 1955, it is evident that little had changed. The shed's roof and sand drier remain, but a standard repair shop has replaced the alfresco hoist just visible in the picture above. The cramped nature of the site led to the coal stage and 35,000 gallon tank being positioned at an angle to the coaling road, so the single tip is itself angled, to compensate. Because of this angularity, expansion of the stage was not possible, but a further tip is visible in the retaining wall between the stage and shed. This unique arrangement was fed by normal skips, charged from the coal stack behind the retaining wall. It appears there was a shortage of labour at Taunton in those days, to judge by the amount of uncleared ash lying around.

Author's Collection & W Potter

Plate 268: When the old Airfix Company sought a typical branch line engine shed on which to base a plastic kit model, they finally chose Tetbury. This quintessence of a GWR small depot shared with Cirencester the distinction of being a sub-shed of Gloucester, but having its engines supplied by Swindon. Tetbury Shed is seen here on 7th August 1950, sixty years old and with another fourteen to go, before closure. To judge by the new brickwork, the water tank had been raised at some time.

T.J. Edgington

Plates 269 & 270: Tiverton Junction's first shed is thought to have opened in 1848, with the branch line from Tiverton. It also supplied engines for the other branch, to Hemyock, and for banking to Whiteball Summit. The shed is distantly visible in the centre of the top picture, an admittedly imperfect print, dating perhaps, from the early years of the 20th century. Track widening and station reconstruction caused the depot's demolition and replacement in 1932, by the building seen below. This was the last branch line shed to be erected by the GWR, and was destined to close in October 1964, three years after the photograph was taken.

Author's Collection & W.T. Stubbs Collection

Plates 271 to 273: Tondu was the junction of the Ogmore Valley and Llynvi & Ogmore Railways, and each had a shed there by the late 1860s. Replacement of those sheds came in 1889, when the GWR installed a Dean single turntable shed in the triangle of lines just north of the station. The top picture, dating from about 1900, partly shows the 'northlight' roofed shed from the station, with the line to Maesteg on the left, and that to Ogmore Vale, and other places, on the right. Note the tall signals, to enable visibility over the depot roof, the highest part of which enclosed a repair shop. At the centre, very early in BR days, No. 4404's driver poses in front of his engine, which is in green livery, with 'British Railways' in GWR-style lettering, GWR buffer beam number, and 'TDU' painted on the cylinder. The 'northlight' roof still existed, but BR were to replace this in 1953, with a loftier asbestos-clad version, having less ridges and large ventilators. The new roof is clearly visible below, on 14th July 1962, seventeen months before Tondu Shed closed, when No. 6436 was paying a visit, some way from her Merthyr home.
*Author's Collection, S. Rickard &
T.W. Nicholls*

Plate 274: Trawsfynydd Shed was opened in 1883, by the Bala & Festiniog Railway, who adopted the simple expedient of adding a lean-to building on the side of a goods shed. This gave the GWR what was probably the most rudimentary of all its locomotive depots. The shed is seen above, four months before closure, on 11th September 1960, with the weekend resident, No. 4683, 'locked in' by a brake van.

W.T. Stubbs Collection

Plate 275: Everything about the South Wales valleys is epitomised in this late 19th century view of the upper Vale of the Rhondda, with Treherbert in the foreground. The collieries, miner's houses, hills, and the railway, can all be seen, as can Treherbert's unusual semi-roundhouse. Erected by the TVR in 1866, it had seven covered and three open radiating roads, and would be replaced in 1931, by a depot erected on the area of open ground visible on the right-hand edge of the picture.

L&GRP, Courtesy of David & Charles

Plate 276: Treherbert's 1931 'Loans Act' shed, on 25th August 1935, with the usual batch of 0-6-2Ts and one Class H Pwllyrhebog shunter. Few changes would be made during the service life of the depot, which closed in March 1965.

B. Matthews

Plate 277: Less than two months before nationalisation, Treherbert's No. 5611 carries a non-standard looking 'GWR' as it stands beside the coal stage. British Railways would later add a small extension to the coaling floor, immediately above the locomotive's front half.

W. Potter

Plates 278 & 279: Tyseley opened as the GWR's main Birmingham depot in 1908. A Churchward double turntable unit, it replaced a 53 year old depot at Bordesley Junction (a shed that has so far eluded the author, photographically). In the top picture, Tyseley is seen from the rear, in July 1939. The line of Pannier tanks is occupying part of the space reserved for a further two turntables — an expedient that never was resorted to. Below, No. 9730 poses beside Tyseley's large double-sided coal stage and 145,000 gallon tank, on 16th August 1939. After the depot's closure in November 1966, this structure became the nucleus of today's Birmingham Railway Museum and the initial home of preserved 4-6-0s No. 7029 *Clun Castle* and LMS No. 5593 *Kolhapur.*

W. Potter & D.K. Jones

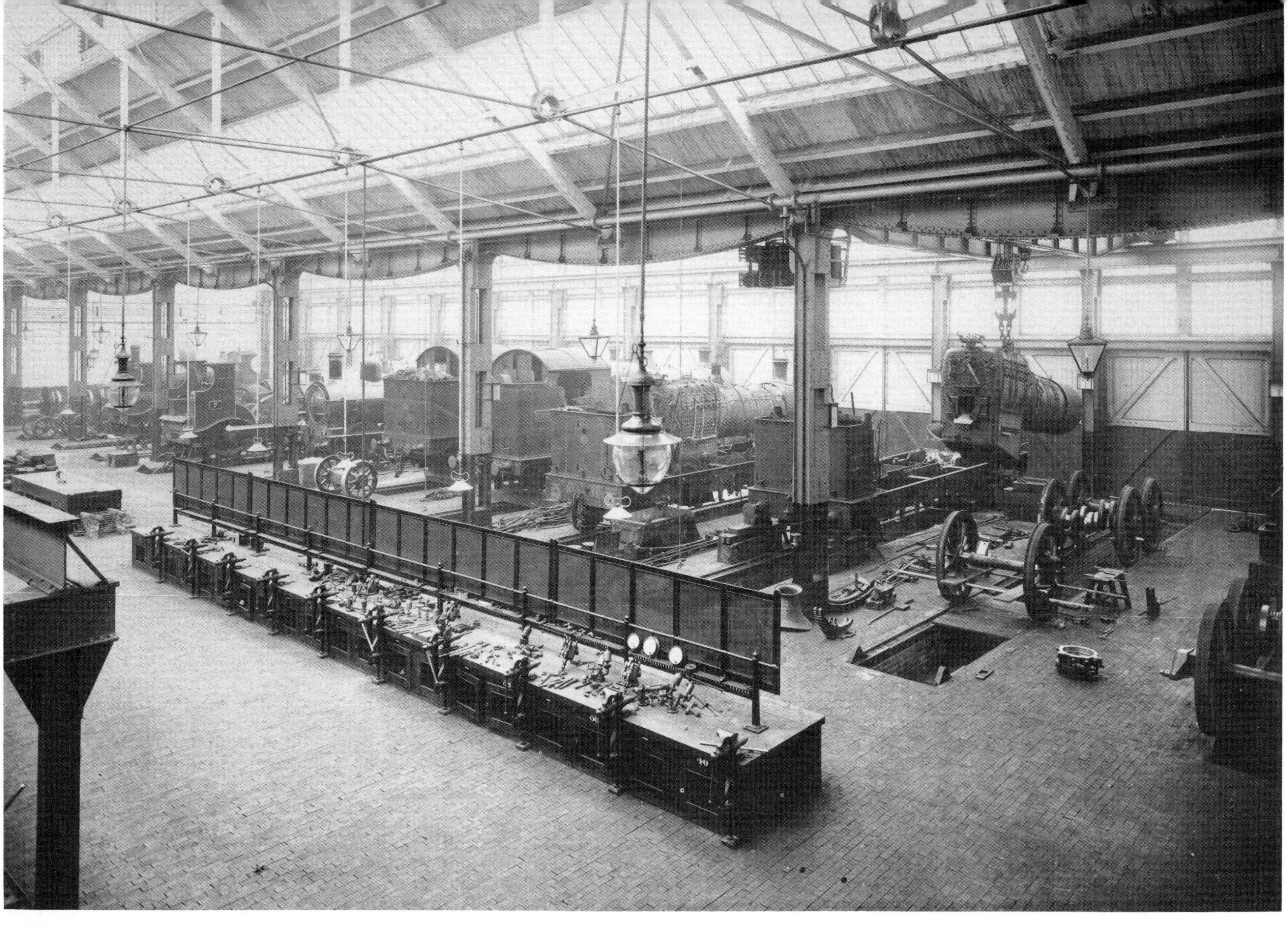

Plate 280: With twelve roads, Tyseley's repair shop was similar in size to that provided at Old Oak Common. This busy scene was captured in 1910, when eight engines, of seven classes, were receiving attention.

BR/OPC

Plate 281: An archetypal Great Western branch line scene, at Wallingford, on 24th October 1953. No. 1444 was working the push-pull branch services to Cholsey (known locally as the 'Bunk'), and would rest overnight in the little loco shed on the left. This was Wallingford's second shed, opened in 1890, to replace the 1866 depot of the Wallingford & Watlington Railway, yet another company whose route aspirations were never to be fully realised. There was an element of idiosyncracy with this depot, as although it was a sub-shed of Didcot, which provided the staff of two drivers, two firemen and a shedman, Wallingford's locomotives were supplied by Reading! This neat little shed closed in 1956, but stood for some years after, in private use.

B. Hilton

Plate 282: The shed at Wellington (Shropshire) opened in the mid-1870s, probably superseding an earlier Shrewsbury & Birmingham Railway depot. It is seen below, circa 1928, with period roof still intact, and 'Stella' Class No. 3201 in commendable condition, probably for working into the heart of LNWR territory, at Crewe. Apart from the Crewe line, Wellington provided engines for local services to Shrewsbury and Wolverhampton, and for the branches radiating from Buildwas; there were sub-sheds at Much Wenlock and Crewe.

W. Potter

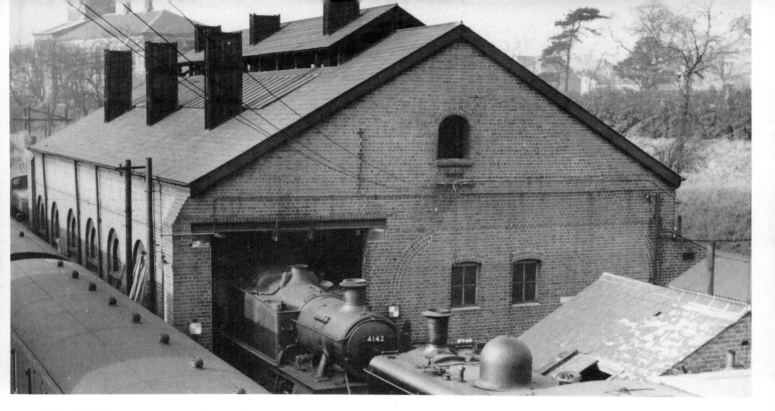

Plate 283: Some sources opine that Wellington loco shed was converted from a goods shed, but the author does not wholly accept that idea. For example, in the 10th November 1957 picture (above), the eastern end of the shed clearly displays that it probably once had three arched openings; the remains of two are visible in the brickwork, while the third now has a steel lintel. The arches might have been decorative window surrounds, as in the side wall, but they are placed higher than those at the side, which points to their once having been doorways, with clearance for locomotives to pass through.

K. Fairey

Plate 284: Wellington's coal stage on a wet and miserable 13th November 1948. A grimy small-wheeled Prairie, No. 4406, still carries a 'WLN' allocation stencil as she simmers in the rain, gaining only partial shelter from the stage's sagging canopy. A gantry type coaler would replace this ageing edifice before the August 1964 closure of the shed.

W. Potter

Plate 285: Although one of Britain's smallest cities, Wells sported loco sheds of the Somerset Central, East Somerset, Bristol & Exeter and Great Western Railways, at varying times, over the years from 1859 to 1963. The depot seen here, near the East Somerset station, was the last to open, in 1879, when the GWR replaced the ESR shed on the same site. The depot office is visible on the right with, on the left, looking towards the shed, a store, sand furnace and water tank, with coal platform and crane beneath; a 55ft. turntable, behind the camera, completed the facilities. This little 'northlight' shed closed in November 1963, four and a half years after this picture was taken.

A.G. Ellis Collection

Plate 286: Later to become one of the Great Western's few narrow gauge involvements, the 2ft. 6in. Welshpool & Llanfair Light Railway opened in 1903. A loco shed was provided at Welshpool for the line's two locomotives and it is depicted here, in July 1949, with No. 822 *The Earl* standing outside. As is well-known, the W&LLR closed in 1956, but both locomotives, and most of the route, survive today, in the expert care of a preservation society. The locoshed, however, was never resurrected.

T.J. Edgington

Plate 287 & 288: The Cambrian Railways provided a two-road engine shed at Welshpool's (standard gauge) station in 1861. The life-expired building was removed around the mid-1930's, but locomotives continued to stable on one open pit, and use the remaining facilities. This may be appreciated above, in June 1951, when 'Dukedog' No. 9012 was photographed when revolving on Welshpoool's 45ft. turntable. The stabling point was officially closed in 1954, but engines continued to stand there for some time after, as seen in the picture below, which shows No. 3209 parked on the remaining shed road on 21st May 1961.

B. Hilton & W.T. Stubbs Collection

Plate 289: A four-road broad gauge shed opened at Westbourne Park in March 1855, replacing the Polygon Shed at Paddington station. A second building, of three roads, was erected in 1862, to cater for 'narrow' (i.e. standard) gauge engines, this being extended to six roads in 1873. With the demise of the broad gauge, the 1855 building was adapted for standard gauge locomotives and it is distantly seen in that condition, in this photograph, which dates from around 1900. The two three-road sections of the 1862/73 shed are at the left, and it is evident that the appellations 'narrow' and 'broad' were still in use, with 'NG1' denoting track one in the 'narrow' gauge building. When Old Oak Common's quadruple turntable shed was completed in 1906, Westbourne Park closed, and its site was later used for a goods depot.

Author's Collection

Plate 290: Presumably visiting under the auspices of the GWR/GCR Joint agreement, Great Central Class 9H (LNER Class J10) No. 837 is pictured outside the former broad gauge shed at Westbourne Park, circa 1900. This engine was built in 1897 by Beyer Peacock and Co. (Works No. 3755), and survived until December 1956, being withdrawn as No. 65162. It may be assumed, perhaps, that the smartly attired gentlemen 'posers' are GCR men, proudly showing off their steed to the rival enginemen.

J. Hooper Collection

Plate 291: Westbury had a small engine shed for a time, during the years 1848 to 1863, being closed because it was surplus to requirements. The eventual creation of the Berks & Hants line as the GWR's main West of England route gave Westbury new prominence, and a Churchward four-road depot was opened in 1915, destined to serve for just over 50 years. That building is seen above, in 1961, showing the lifting shop on the right-hand side, with boiler house in front. From the layout of the sidings on the left, it is obvious that provision had been made for the depot's expansion, but as in virtually all other instances, this never came about.

C.L. Caddy

Plate 292: The ornate stonework of Weston-super-Mare's small shed is an indicator to its age. Erected in 1861 by the B&ER, this building replaced an earlier shed which was itself built when locomotives took over from the horse-power initially used on the branch. The depot could be very busy during the summer months, when there was much holiday traffic; in fact, an excursion station was built to deal with it, and this is just visible behind No. 4075 *Cardiff Castle*. The picture dates from 22nd August 1952, eight years before the shed closed, and some twenty five years before the M5 motorway finally killed off the railway's summer carryings. Today, the site of the shed and Locking Road excursion station is covered by a superstore and, of course, car-parks.

A.R. Goult

Plate 293: The oldest picture in the album, this extraordinary photograph shows Weymouth broad gauge shed in 1857, the year of its opening. In fact, construction work was still in progress to the left of the water tank. One or two standard gauge tracks are also visible; these were LSWR lines, of course, and that company had an engine shed opposite the GWR building, out of the picture, to the right. This unique study was the work of one William Thompson, of Weymouth, a remarkable man who is also credited with having taken the world's first underwater photograph, in 1856! His pioneering loco shed photograph is reproduced here by kind permission of Mrs R. Kynaston Thompson, widow of William Thompson's great-grandson.

Plate 294: Weymouth's broad gauge shed closed in June 1885, to be succeeded by a three-road Dean 'northlight' depot, on a new site. This shed received a single-pitch gable roof in the 1930s, and that is seen here in June 1955 (centre). Despite the fact that Southern Railway/ Region engines used the depot from 1938, this picture has a solidly Great Western atmosphere, apart from one Standard Class 5 4-6-0. That, and the placidity of the scene, are due to the picture having been taken during the 1955 ASLEF strike. The shed closed in July 1967.

J. Lucking

Plates 295 & 296:   Whitland's first engine shed was opened about 1863, by the Pembroke & Tenby Railway. It burned down and was replaced by the GWR, during 1901/2. With economy in mind, the GWR utilised an ex-contractor's loco shed from Letterston, erected there in 1894, for the construction of the North Pembrokeshire & Fishguard Railway. Naturally, such a building would be somewhat temporary in nature and, by the mid-1930s (above), it was showing definite signs of wear and tear! No. 2440 was resident on that day, one of the normal allocation of about 15 locomotives. When the GWR renovated the building around 1939/40, wartime conditions forced continued economy, resulting in a further corrugated iron structure, with an improved yard layout. Still in good condition, the refurbished shed is seen below on 4th May 1952, with Nos 2288, 1601 and 5677 visible. Note that the 36ft. turntable outside the shed entrance has been removed and replaced by an ash pit; however the little wooden office and coaling canopy are the same. The shed remained in this condition until closed, in January 1966.

B. Matthews & W. Potter

Plate 297: The area around Wolverhampton (Stafford Road) had a complex history, with a Shrewsbury & Birmingham, and two Great Western sheds in close proximity, by 1854. Eventually, all activity centred on the GWR depot that started with a four-road broad gauge building. A turntable shed for standard gauge engines was added in 1860, with the four-road building being extended alongside, and the gap between the two sheds becoming a further straight shed, of two roads. Around 1874/5, two further turntable sheds were erected and there development rested, until the coming of railmotors, when a four-road straight shed, 275ft. long, was provided for their use. That exhausted the site's expansion capabilities and all buildings had reached an advanced state of decrepitude by the time closure came, in September 1963. With such a complicated location only an aerial photograph can put things in perspective, as here, in a view dating from 31st May 1939. In the left foreground is Stafford Road Shed, with the largest section of roof covering the three turntables; from the left are Nos 1, 2 (with roof partly missing) and 3. Below these, to the right, between the coal stack and LNWR embankment, is the railmotor shed, by then in other use, as was turntable shed No. 3, to judge by the lack of smoke vents. Just seen, at the top left of the turntable building are the two-road and four-road straight shed sections, with various works buildings beyond. The depot's coal stage and external 64ft. turntable are also visible, remotely sited on the other side of the LNWR viaduct. In the triangle formed by Stafford Road, the main line, and the spur to Victoria Basin, are further old works buildings, some of which stand on the site of the former S&B loco shed. Opposite can be seen the triple-pitched roof of the 1932 Works building, which covered the site of the second of the GWR's original depots — a two-road straight shed. Lastly, in the upper left distance, between the golf and race courses, are Oxley marshalling yard and double turntable shed.

Aerofilms

Plates 298 & 299: The straight sheds at Wolverhampton (Stafford Road) are shown here, with the top picture probably dating from about the mid-1880s. The four-road shed is seen at left, with doors closed and 'live' engines parked outside. On the right are rows of tenders and locomotives awaiting repair in the various shops to the right of, and behind, the loco shed. Below, is a June 1938 picture of the four and two-road straight sheds, still with their original roofs — both were later reclad in corrugated iron. The first broad gauge shed formed the rear section of the four-road building and, just visible on the left, is one of the transverse pitches of the roof over No. 2 turntable. A 2-6-2T locomotive No. 4114, and 4-6-0s Nos 5921 *Bingley Hall* and 4067 *Tintern Abbey*, are among the engines seen.

Woodfin Collection, courtesy of Bristol City Museum & W. Potter.

Plates 300 & 301: Views of Stafford Road's turntable sheds. Above, on 11th October 1933, 'Barnum' class No. 3223 and 0-6-0PT No. 1524 stand outside the southern entrance to No. 2 turntable shed, with the roof over No. 1 beyond. To judge by the coal tipped on the ground, both engines had been readied for workshops attention — probably the last such visit for No. 3223, as she was to be withdrawn in May 1936 (the pannier followed, three years later). Note the old-fashioned rail still in use. A view inside No. 2 shed (below) in June 1938, shows assorted engines grouped around the 40ft. turntable. Notice again the U-section rails and the somewhat rudimentary method of interleaving two lines — the short check rail looks very flimsy!

G. Coltas & W. Potter

Plates 302 & 303: The main depot of the OW&WR, Worcester, opened in 1852, and would appear to have comprised two buildings from very early on. From the well-known 'Railway Walk' vantage point, come these two prints, with that above dating from about 1910. By tradition, the three-road building housed passenger engines, while goods locomotives frequented the four-road shed. Note the neat coal stack on the left and, across the Wolverhampton line, Worcester Works, with Shrub Hill Station in the far distance. The line to Hereford passes behind the two buildings, over the steeply-graded 'Vinegar Branch', while the double track seen at bottom of the picture completes the triangle, with a direct connection from Foregate Street Station to the Wolverhampton route. By 1964 (below) there was little evidence of any alteration, except to the building roofs, and lines of spare locomotives replacing coal wagons between the sheds. Worcester Depot closed to steam in December 1965, but vestiges of both buildings survive today, as part of a mixed diesel stabling point/civil engineer's yard.

A.G. Ellis Collection & C.L. Caddy

Plates 304 & 305: Worcester's very tidy coal stack is shown again above, circa 1929, with 'Bulldog' No. 3313 *Jupiter*, in the foreground. As can be seen, the depot had, by that time, two steam-powered coaling cranes. That on the left, with canopy, was obviously the regular appliance, with the open-air machine being used as standby for breakdowns, or periods of high demand. Such high demand eventually led to the replacement of the standby crane by an automated device. This is seen below, on 8th October 1949, with yet another 'Bulldog', No. 3453 *Seagull* — by that time, one of the few remaining members of the class — posing in front. The skip-hoist coaling plant was actually provided in 1944, and only one other of its type was to be installed at Southall, in 1954.

Lens of Sutton & W. Potter

Plate 306: Recent scene, very old subject! Locomotive Department hand crane No. 340, as found inside the roofless four-road former loco shed at Worcester on 11th August 1979. Does any reader know of the crane's fate?

J.A. Sommerfield

Plates 307 & 308: Yatton's engine shed opened in 1879 and may have been the re-erection of Clevedon loco shed, removed when the station there was enlarged. For working the Clevedon and Wells branches, Yatton normally had an allocation of about three locomotives, and one of these, a GWR-liveried Class 1400 0-4-2T, is seen on shed, in the top picture, on 13th February 1949. The small office building is obviously a late addition and its resident staff seem to have ensured themselves a good supply of fresh eggs! Exactly eleven years later, less one day (below) the chickens had gone, snow lay on the ground, and despite the fact that Yatton Depot would be closed in another six months, some roof retiling work was in progress. The inside and outside locomotive pits are clearly seen, while the left-hand interior wall displays what seems, for such a small shed, an inordinate amount of notice board space!

T.J. Edgington & W.R. Dyer Collection

ACKNOWLEDGEMENTS

When my friend, John Hooper, who produced *LMS* and *LNER Sheds in Camera* for OPC, suggested I should compile a similar volume on GWR sheds, my initial reaction was one of euphoria. I could indulge myself in my favourite railway and my favourite subject, locosheds, simultaneously! Only later did the doubts set in, because it was the Great Western — hadn't every word been written, every picture been seen?

I need not have worried — for that very reason — i.e. because it *WAS* the Great Western, and therefore the most popular of Britain's railways by far. Such popularity has ensured that numerous previously untapped sources of photographs remain. So, after the almost impossible job of deciding which material to leave out, finding the words was a pleasant, relatively simple task.

This brings me to words of gratitude to the many people who so willingly allowed me to use their photographs. Their names are given below, but a few I must mention separately, as without their special help, this book could not have existed. I first refer specifically to Bill Potter, whose prolific camera work from the 1930s, and collection of earlier material, yielded nearly a quarter of the pictures used in this album. Next is Bernard Matthews, for his own vintage works and whose skill today, in unearthing old prints, borders on the supernatural! Then come Bill Stubbs and Brian Hilton, both old friends, and custodians of large photographic collections, in addition to their own marvellous works. Last, but by no means least, my good pal and fellow Bristolian, Terry Nicholls, ever the photographer first, and railway enthusiast second — his record of his former workplace, Laira is, I hope given an exposure worthy of its quality.

Several works of reference were of inestimable value in the preparation of this album, and I have already alluded to Messrs E. Lyons and E. Mountford's books on GWR loco sheds. This leaves that masterpiece which no student of GW locomotive affairs would be without. I refer, of course, to *The Locomotives of the GWR*, published in 13 parts by the Railway Correspondence & Travel Society, of which it has been my pleasure to be a member for the past quarter of a century. Then, for recent information, I am grateful to Nick Pigott, Steve Dymond and Stephen Hillman of the Engine Shed Society, and the Society's journal "Link".

For support, my thanks go to Noel Bell and all those at OPC, for agreeing to my compiling the book so far from Britain's shores, with all the added complications that entailed. Finally, but most important of all, my loving thanks go to my wife Jane, for her seemingly limitless reserves of patience and understanding, for the many hours I spent isolated with a word processor and piles of photographs. To you all goes my deepest gratitude.

THE PHOTOGRAPHERS

Colin Caddy
Bill Camwell
Hubert Casserley
Gordon Coltas
Ron Dyer
John Edgington
Bruce Ellis (A. G. Ellis Collection)
Ken Fairey
E. V. Fry
A. R. Goult
Brian Green
John Hooper
Keith Jones

Aerofilms
Bristol City Museum (Woodfin Collection)
British Rail
L & GRP (David & Charles Ltd)

L. B. Lapper
John Lucking
Brian Miller (and the Welsh Railways Research Circle)
Cedric Owen
Jim Peden
Norman Preedy
Sid Rickard
Allan Sommerfield
Hamish Stevenson
Peter Tatlow
Mrs Rosemary Thompson
Tony Wright
W. H. Whitworth

Lens of Sutton
OPC
Railprint (BR/OPC) Joint Venture